Champion Your Career

Winning in the World of Work

By Halimah Bellows, MA, MS, CCC, CPC

Champion Your Career
Seattle, Washington
www.championyourcareer.com_

ISBN: 978-1-5136-0613-2

To order additional copies, please contact:

hbellows@championyourcareer.com

DEDICATION

This book is dedicated to my mother, Rosalind Mona Bellows, my best friend and greatest supporter, who was a true diva, who charmed and inspired everyone she knew especially me. Her words of wisdom have never been forgotten and have influenced me on the many paths I have taken in my life. Her favorite words to me were, "If there is a will, there is a way. If you want to, you can do it, and there is no such word as can't." That's how this book came to be.

Thanks Mom

To Paul: 8/12/16

Already a champion in his career & for others. Keep on winning in the world of work & life.

Love

[signature]

ACKNOWLEDGEMENTS:

First and foremost I wish to thank and acknowledge my clients whose career paths I have been fortunate enough to play a part in. Your successes and willingness to follow your dreams and pursue your passions is what has inspired me to continue with the work that I do.

This book would not have come to be had it not been for Dr. Pat Bacilli, whose idea it was and who gave me the rights to the radio script, to turn my 10 week radio show into a book and a deck of cards. The deck of cards came first, now the book. Thanks Dr. Pat.

Many thanks also go to my family, friends and colleagues, who each read chapters and gave me their comments as well as encouragement to keep going. A big thank you to my first editor Linda Hurst who started the process of turning the radio scripts into prose. And finally, thank you, thank you, thank you ad infinitum to my developmental editor Julie Fretzin. Without her help, unwavering patience (with me) and the writing process, as well as her stellar writing and editing skills, this book would not have happened. Again, Thank you everyone who played a part in the creation of this book.

To my readers I wish you success in finding work that is right for you and in championing your career. I know you can be a winner in the world of work.

CONTENTS

CHAPTER 1: FOCUS ON YOUR FUTURE

I remember standing in the cafeteria line at school when I was nine years old when, occasionally, other children would come up and talk to me and tell me their stories. I didn't ask them to; I was just standing there, waiting in line for my food. They would start telling me everything about themselves or what their problems were, and I would respond with something like, "Wow, I can hear you've had a really hard time," or, "I hear that you're in a lot of pain," or something like that. And then they would talk some more.

I think I just had this gift, a natural ability that drew others to come and talk to me and to tell me their problems. Somehow they knew I would listen and that I would be non-judgmental. This natural ability followed me the rest of my life in the careers that I have chosen—as an educator, career counselor, and coach. I have always wanted to listen to and be of service to others. People have always fascinated me and the world of work fascinates me as well. By marrying the two as a career counselor/coach, I bring together my innate abilities and passions and the skills that have naturally flowed from me since I was a child.

This experience has given me the special joy that comes from championing the causes of other people and providing support that can help them discover new aspects of themselves, while watching them expand and develop. Life is full of obstacles and there are times when we all need someone to champion us; to be in our corner to cheer us on and guide us in finding effective solutions to our problems. Sometimes, however, we have to do that ourselves.

Become Your Own Career Champion

This book is designed to help you understand that you have the power to be your own champion. You can create your own positive perspective with the messages you play in your inner dialogue and then manifest those messages in the material world. You can do this for yourself. Do not allow other people to tell you, "Don't do this" or "You shouldn't do that" or "This is not good enough." Instead, you can say, "I know what works for me. I can make my own life and I can champion my career. I can make it happen for myself. I can be successful at whatever vocation I choose."

As you move through this process you will see that when you show up to work, you get to decide how your situation is going to be. There are no victims in the career development ladder unless you choose to be one. The inner voice that says, "I have to get a job," gradually shifts to be more about, "I want to do something that feels good to me, something that serves me. I want to be in an environment that's nurturing and productive."

Career Development Theory

The theory of career development has not changed over the many years I have been doing this work. To answer the question "What career is right for you?" there are three important answers to seek out:

1. What are your interests? What do you love to do?
2. What are your values—professional as well as personal?
3. What are your skills and talents?

All of the career tests, assessments and services are designed to determine this fundamental information.

Defining Your Interests

One way to develop a strategy for finding work that meets your fundamental goals is to take a very close look at where your interests lie. To help define them, you can try this assessment developed by Richard Bowles, the author of the popular *What Color Is Your Parachute?* It's based on the

Holland Code, which was created by John Holland and is the basis for such governmental resources as the *Dictionary of Occupational Titles* and the *Occupational Outlook Handbook*.

The Holland Code describes a process by which all people and all jobs can be divided into six distinct categories. The model is drawn as a hexagon with the categories placed in a specific order. Beginning with the top and continuing in a clockwise pattern, the six categories are:

1. **R**ealistic: Athletes and mechanical people who prefer to work with objects, plants or animals, or like to be outdoors.
2. **I**nvestigative: Scientists, people who like to observe, analyze and solve problems.
3. **A**rtistic: Artists and musicians, innovative, creative and those who like unstructured environments.
4. **S**ocial: People who work with people; teachers, guides, counselors. They care and they are very good with words.
5. **E**nterprising: Managers, influencers, persuaders, lawyers.
6. **C**onventional: People who like to work with data in a systematic way. They are numerical, have clerical ability, and pay attention to detail.

Holland Code Model

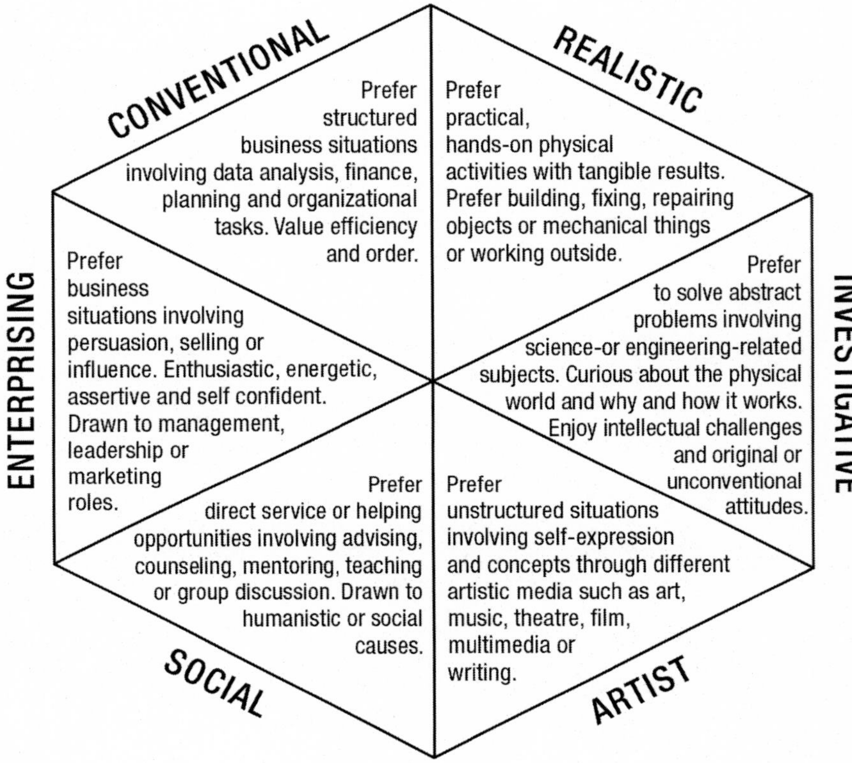

This exercise allows us to understand our work preferences based on the six categories. The exercise begins as you imagine that you are at a party where people from these six categories are grouped together around the room. Notice which group you are drawn to join first. Imagine spending time with these people and see how that feels. Now see which group you would be drawn to next and imagine spending time with them. Repeat one more time so that you have chosen the three groups you were most attracted to.

Now you have a three-letter code based on the first letter of each group (in the order you chose them). Your code might be R-I-A, A-S-C, I-E-C, or any of the other possibilities. We seek people like us. If you are an entrepreneurial type, you are probably going to want to spend more of your time in that kind of environment and with those kinds of people. Careers work the same way. So once you determine your code, you can research the industries, jobs, companies and people that are associated with your code and with each category. This book will show you how to do this research.

Obviously, this is a very simplified version of the assessment process but it is definitely a way to get started. This is a self-directed assessment and there are no right or wrong answers. Keep in mind, however, that the categories that are right next to each other in the hexagon are most compatible. It is going to be easier and more straightforward to find a career that marries two or all three of them. With two types on the opposite ends of the hexagon, such as a C and an A, you are going to have a harder time finding work that is satisfying to you. Maybe you will find work that satisfies one category and decide to develop the other interest outside of work time.

No job is going to give you 100 percent of what you want, but my advice is to aim for at least 70 percent job satisfaction. The latter is a really good figure and you could be quite happy with that level of career-related fulfillment. When the figure starts to go down to 50 percent job satisfaction, it means that half the time something is not right, something is out of place. Remember this is half of your workday. You then must start looking honestly at your situation and determine if you are "stuck" in the job.

Some people might make the decision to accept a 50 percent satisfaction level from their work life, because perhaps they happily leave their job at the office and then come home and pursue a hobby like playing music. You need to look at your own workday to determine if you are able to make a 50 percent job satisfaction work for you, or if you feel you are stuck in a dead-end situation.

As you know, you have two sides of your life: your work life and your personal life. What you should aim for is to blend the two together to come up with a TOTAL satisfaction level. If your work life and your personal life do not add up to a high enough level of satisfaction, then you might be ready to look at a career change. Either way, this book will help you determine what your basic needs are for happiness in the workplace, as well as your personal life. Then it will help you move on to a higher level of overall satisfaction in your life.

A Note for College Students

In the past, it was normal for students to declare a major related to a career, complete a prescribed set of studies, find a job in a related field, and stay in that field until they retired. One decision and that was it! Today, however, it is far more common for students to change their majors and do several career searches and changes in their work lifetime.

People change their careers for a variety of reasons. Perhaps they made an unwise choice initially or the career they selected no longer exists. Often they want to match their changing values and needs to a new set of career possibilities.

Making the right plans for your future during these changing times can be difficult. The self-assessment tools provided in this book can give you more choices, broaden your options, and give you the confidence that you are on the right career path.

A self-assessment can reveal your characteristics, interests, values and skills. It will define your strengths and your weaknesses. Looking for a match between these and the work you are considering is the most important step you can take before you write a résumé or begin your job search. In fact, when the time comes to write your résumé and prepare for a job interview, you will find the task easier if you have completed the self-assessment process first!

Recognizing the Need for Change

If you are already working, there are three main reasons why a career change might be right for you. First, it could be that you have the right job with the wrong company. For example, you may love the work you do as an administrative assistant, but you may not like the philosophy of the company, or you may find that you cannot stand behind their mission. Their values are not a match for yours. If the environment, including the people, is not a good fit for you, even the right work you do will feel like you're in the wrong job.

The second reason could be that you have the wrong position in the right company. In this case, you should look at your passions, interests and skills and find a way to put them to use in your own position or in another job within the same company. For some people, it might be about finding time outside of work to make use of those skills.

The third reason that career change might be right for you is that job security is an illusion. You might love your job and your company, but the company could move, reorganize, or go out of business due to various unforeseeable circumstances. This is why determining your skills and talents is such an important strategy in career development—no matter where you go, you take those skills and talents with you.

In this book, we'll delve into identifying your interests, values and skills, and then provide you with the concrete tools to choose, develop and change your career, no matter what stage of life you are currently in. These will include networking, goal-setting, researching, and decision-making. Sections are dedicated to writing résumés, cover letters and follow-up letters, as well as appropriate dress attire and other interview strategies.

Students will find specific guidance for launching a new career after college. Retirees will learn how to retire with fire by enlivening their retirement years with work they are passionate about. So get ready to champion your career!

CHAPTER 2: CHANGE CAREERS WITH COURAGE

Any kind of change takes courage. People want to stay where they are comfortable. However, in order for you to be truly satisfied throughout your work life, your career needs to change and grow with you.

Your Holland Code—the three job categories you are most attracted to—may change throughout your life. In fact, they most likely *will* change. Statistics show that people change careers up to three times throughout their lives—and some people pursue as many as seven careers. We are different people at age 20 than we are at age 30, 40, 50 or 60. We look at life differently and our values change too.

That is why identifying your values is such a key part of career development. This process involves asking and answering questions of yourself about what is important to you, and observing what you feel passionately attracted to (as well as what you feel passionately *repelled* by).

10 Reasons for Pursuing Your Ideal Career

I have a short list of the top 10 reasons why you need to work at having your dream job. These reasons will be reaffirmed throughout this book as you read on.

Reason #1: If you are doing what you love to do, it allows you to be your true self all of the time. Think about it. It really takes a tremendous amount of energy on a daily basis to not be authentic at work. Sometimes we feel we have to take on a sort of "false persona" to fulfill the job requirements. Your ideal job will enable you to be who you are and not waste any energy.

Reason #2: Your dream job fits into your life by integrating perfectly into your lifestyle. Your ideal career will feel like a natural part of who you are and it will not necessarily interfere with other aspects of your life. Of course, some days may be more stressful and chaotic than others, but basically you can still find the balance to have a fulfilling life.

Reason #3: Your ideal career reflects and incorporates your values. Your values reflect what is truly important to you and your dream career will align with the values that resonate with you. For example, if you are concerned about the environment, your dream job is not going to ask you to be involved with toxic waste dumping. It is as simple as that: Living your values. You are going to love your work and it is going to give you what you want in order to feel alive and productive.

Reason #4: Your dream job will allow you to tap into your unique talents. Your skills and strengths are gifts that come naturally to you. If you are in your ideal career, it will feel like a perfect fit. It will allow you to express yourself fully and you will notice that your work will feel effortless.

Reason #5: Your work will give you energy instead of draining you. If you're not doing work that's right for you, you will probably feel drained and tired when you come home. But if you're doing what you love, you will feel energized by it instead of exhausted by it. You'll look forward to it. You will embrace it every day. And if you receive energy from your work, this will energize other areas of your life as well.

Reason #6: Your dream career will enable you to align yourself with your passions and to do what you love. This is a core component of the right livelihood. When you're passionate about what you do, your purpose is fulfilled and you will feel very satisfied and comfortable. Then you become a more generous, caring human being.

Reason #7: Your dream job helps you to make a difference in something you believe in. Generally, when you do what you love, you believe in it. You want to do more of it. You feel you are making a difference and you feel happy about doing this work. Sometimes you'll think about your work and it will bring about change in your life or help to clarify something else that's important to you.

Reason #8: Of course your ideal career is enjoyable and it does not seem like work. Very frequently, if you love what you do, you're going to wake up in the morning and say, "Do I really get paid for doing this?" Your dream job can feel more like a hobby than a job!

Reason #9: A dream job follows your wants instead of your "shoulds." You're listening to your intuition and to your heart instead of solely to your rational mind. When you listen to what your intuition says, then you will find that the rest of your life will start to rearrange itself so that you can truly be who you are and enjoy a truly meaningful life.

Reason #10: Your dream job fulfills you. It gives a sense of completion. You will have a positive impact on others and your community because you are serving your own life's purpose.

Fantasy Workday

Here's an exercise to help you consider your most compelling dreams. Close your eyes and try to imagine the ideal workday for yourself. Don't be concerned with the realities—just let your imagination go. See if you can picture, in full detail, what you would be doing. Then open your eyes and answer the following questions.

When done, go back over your answers and put an "I"' for those you feel are indispensable, an "O" for those that are desirable but optional, and an "F" for those which are basically a frill.

- You wake up—at what time?
- You get dressed—describe your clothes.
- What kind of preparations do you have to make?
- Do you have to work or do you work because you want to?
- How do you get there? How far is it?
- Do you do anything special on the way to work?
- You get to work. Where are you (city, small town, office park, home, etc.)?

- Describe the work setting.
- What kind of work do you do?
- What is the first task that you attend to as you start your day?
- What skills do you use and enjoy using today?
- What are the people like in your organization?
- How long have you worked there?
- What do you get paid?
- What are your benefits?
- What level is the job (professional, training, management, technical, apprenticeship)?
- Do you plan your work or does someone do it for you? How do you work (alone, in a group, contact with others)?
- Describe the people who work in your area.
- To whom do you report?
- Is it a quiet or busy setting? What is the pace like? Is it the same throughout the day or does it vary?
- Is the work predictable or are there changes as the day progresses?
- Is the work project- or process-oriented? What is satisfying about the work?
- How does the time flow? What is the course of the day like?
- What type of supervision are you receiving as you work?
- What do you do at lunchtime? How do you feel?
- What do you like about your job or occupation?
- What is the end of your day like? What happens next?
- Is there carryover between what happens at work and the rest of your life?
- How long do you see yourself remaining at this job?

- What is the next move (job step) for you?
- What are your highest aspirations in this field or place of employment?

Now consider the following questions based on the ideal workday that you have envisioned:

- What do you notice about the overall flow of the day? How is it similar to or different from your current or recent work situation?
- How does this work draw on your strengths and skills?
- How does this work complement the rest of your life? Is it separated from or integrated into your life?
- What does this exercise teach you about yourself? How can you use this information in your career planning?
- What additional information do you need to gather based on this exercise?
- What are the next steps for you now?

Four Stories about People Finding Their Ideal Careers

The following are stories of four different people sharing their successes and struggles to find and commit to their ideal career. They all went through their own unique process of finding their dream work but they all also went through the process of honestly assessing their personal values, interests, skills and talents.

Sara relates how she took small steps toward finding her ideal work situation:

"I had been working for our local arts council and not really happy with my job there. I decided to leave the job and look for work that reflected more of my values and that would utilize my skills and talents. It was important to me that I could really make some kind of impact or be of service in some way to the world. And at the same time, I wanted to have a job that I would feel

passionate about. It was also important for me to work with people of good intention.

"So I'd been thinking about this for a long time. I looked at certain work and I thought, 'No, I can't do this, I can't do that.' I had little jobs here and there. For two years, I didn't have a definite job. I was lucky to own my own home, so I was able to take out a loan. I maxed out my credit cards like a lot of people do but daily and constantly in my heart was this 'Please bring me a job that will use my skills where I can be of benefit to humankind.'

"Eventually, through a friend, I met a man whose work I admired on another radio show. He had a public affairs program, talking about current issues of the day. I always liked his passion, his articulate conversation, his really good energy, so I was kind of a fan of his. One day this man and I were talking and I mentioned that one of my friends works for him. Then I said, 'If ever you need help, please let me know. I'd be really interested to work with you.' About two months later, he contacted me and said, 'One of my employees has left. Are you interested in the job?' Now I currently play world music on local public radio and have been doing so for thirteen years in Northern California.

"It didn't happen overnight. It took two years for it to come to fruition, but through all that time I was networking and making contacts and following up on all opportunities that came my way. I wasn't just sitting around waiting. At the same time, I was *waiting."*

Mary has some struggles in identifying what is important to her apart from significant other aspects of her life. This is her story:

"I'm almost afraid to go for something that I love to do because maybe it would be called impractical and really I have an awful lot of negativity in my life from my upbringing with parents who were really tough on me. I didn't have a lot of self-esteem and I still don't and I think that interferes with giving myself permission to go forward. I just don't know how to overcome that."

Now Mary needs to have a strategy to deal with the "yeah, buts." We in the coaching profession call these negative voices Gremlins. The key is to recognize the negative thoughts as your Gremlins because if you recognize them, you're taking away some of their power. And these voices, these "yeah, buts," want to keep us in homeostasis because it's comfortable there. It's a way of protecting ourselves from getting hurt or from the possibility of failing. But when you notice those voices you can say, "Thank you for noticing. Thank you for telling me this but, you know, I'm going to do it anyway."

So keep listening to these "yeah, buts" and write down what they say to you. Make a list of your own personal "yeah, buts" and start listening to the number of times these "yeah, buts" come up when you start thinking about having your ideal career. Remember to say, "Thank you for your concern but, you know, I'm going to move ahead anyway." Or try to take even a little step to move you towards- what you want. The Gremlin voice may not notice it or care that you've taken these tiny steps forward. Make one call a day about job opportunities instead of thinking you have to do 10 calls. Start slowly and try to be consistent.

As for finding work to pay the bills, sometimes you have to take a job that is not your ideal but that does not mean that you should stop moving toward the job that you want and taking those small steps toward it. The truth of the matter is that when you're looking for work—guess what? It's easier to find a better job when you already have a job. Just keep in mind what it is you really want to do. Again, take your small steps on a daily or weekly basis to achieve your goal and to keep moving forward.

Jenna has this to share about her career search process:

"Consistently writing down my career goals has been so important in my life. Even 10 years ago, when my husband and I got married, I told him, "Honey, I'm not going to work if we have kids." And that was so firmly planted in my thoughts that what came to me about two years later was that I had the ability to be the manager of our property. So the apartment that we were living in ended up coming free to us and all I had to do was carry my little baby with me to answer phone calls and go show apartments and be very talkative

and friendly. I had a job that fit into my lifestyle and I just loved meeting and visiting with people. It was just an extension of myself. And I got paid for it! We didn't have to pay our rent.

"But then I realized that I really didn't have the talent, the skill, but mostly the energy, to homeschool my kids alone. And so my husband and I started having conversations about what I needed in order to find an income that could replace my husband's corporate salary so that he could homeschool our children. We put out this intention and what came to us was starting a brokerage company in which my husband had some background. And the reason it fit so perfectly with us was that we had the ability to make above and beyond the income we ever dreamed of. We could all be together and have the lifestyle we wanted.

"Since we have the earning foundation in place, I have turned to my true passion, which is nutrition. I also work with selling and informing local health food store members about the importance of good nutritional products and I love it! All over my house I have written, 'Reach for the stars because you'll never be bigger than your dreams.'"

Sandy tells her success story about finding her ideal career:

"This is actually a pretty joyful week for me because I just gave notice on a five- year job as a vocational counselor at my local community college. I've moved into my own practice, which has been fourteen years in the making. I'm a counselor and I specialize in helping clients find their career path using several right- and left-brain processes.

"I would say the seeds for this were planted when I was very young. Probably back to the fifth grade when everyone else was reading Mrs. Piggle-Wiggle, *I was reading parapsychology books. And, of course, it never occurred to me that I could make a living with that. I pursued a regular career as a systems analyst. Eventually I earned bachelor's and master's degrees in psychology, and slowly moved into counseling clients after my regular work hours of being a systems analyst.*

"I sent out the seeds in prayer, visions and action steps and my private practice has finally come to fruition. I'm able to be of service to many, many people by helping them bring their insights into a workable vision. My analytical background has also been useful in my current counseling practice. I had to find the courage, in a sense, to commit to a career and to really stick to the commitment of bringing my vision, my passion to reality. It took me about 14 years to get there and it was like step by step by step. And then it came to a point where I said, 'Now is the time.' I am very practical and I really waited until I had enough savings and my own house and all the things in place before I took the leap to quit my daytime job and focused on my private counseling practice. It was helpful also for me to slowly take a leap out of my systems analyst position by asking my employer to decrease my weekly hours."

In reading about these people's challenges and then finding the courage to commit to a career, there are a few principles to remember.

First, these dream jobs didn't happen overnight. Each person went through a process of determining what their values were and set intentions about what kind of work they wanted, where and with whom they wanted to work.

Second, all your 'ducks' do not need to be in a row. Most people who are successful got their first jobs with only a general idea of their career goal and some of the skills required to succeed. Then they moved forward. They may have done it little by little because it is a process of research—but mostly discovering and experiencing—what was truly reflective of their true values, gifts and passions. So you don't have to have everything in place before you make that leap. You can do it slowly. Just remember that not everything needs to be fully known or processed when you're starting to commit to a career. Each step you take brings you closer to your goal, to what you want. The experience you acquire from doing *any* work has value. Although the position may not be your dream job, the skills learned still can be helpful later when you do link up with your ideal career.

We learn something from everything we do. I mean, even when things don't go well, I always ask myself, "Okay, so what's the universe trying to teach me by giving me this experience?" Try not to think about your work life so much as a career but more as an opportunity to grow and to know yourself more fully. Then you can have more fun building your resources with more detachment. If you can view the work of finding your right livelihood as play, as life lessons to be learned, all with an attitude of detachment, then you will be more open to all opportunities—expected and unexpected—that come your way.

I am reminded of a story one client shared with me. She said, "You know, when I was unemployed and I had just moved to a new country and a new city, I didn't know anybody. I was just kind of wondering who I was and what I was worth. And then, oh my goodness, my whole life just opened up for me. I didn't even know what was available to me and I just happened to bump into people who said, 'So, what are you interested in? What do you love to do?' and I didn't even know they would ever offer me a job. But after talking with me for half an hour just about life, they said, 'Would you please come and work for us?'"

My client's story reflects the need to keep networking. She kept putting herself out there, engaging with those who could help her. Her attitude and willingness took her closer to her ideal career.

You have a winning attitude when you can say to yourself and others, "This is an experience I can learn something from." And again, every job gives you certain knowledge of an industry, of people, of certain skills, and you can put it all together to find your ideal job and do what you really love.

Here are some WISE WORDS ABOUT CAREER CHOICES from Abraham Hicks.

"A very good career choice would be to gravitate toward those activities and to embrace those desires that harmonize with your core intentions, which are freedom and growth—and joy. Make a 'career' of living a happy life rather

than trying to find work that will produce enough income that you can do things with your money that will then make you happy. When feeling happy is of paramount importance to you—and what you do 'for a living' makes you happy—you have found the best of all combinations."

CHAPTER 3 : POWER UP YOUR PASSIONS

Passion and Purpose

Purpose relates to finding and sharing our gifts and talents as only we can uniquely express them. Living in passion and purpose is so important to our needs as humans that, without these elements being fulfilled, most people will live empty, meaningless, depressing lives.

Because your work life takes up a significant part of your adult life on a day-to-day basis, it is completely vital to bring your passions and the meaning you give to your life's purpose into your work environment. Defining your purpose is the first step in doing work that you love; work that encourages you to grow as a human being.

In fully uncovering and embracing our passions, we find a deeper purpose that gives a richer meaning to our lives beyond gratification of our egos. A calling is like an organism, a living entity, with a purpose all its own. It drives us toward authenticity and aliveness.

Saying "yes" to a calling tends to place you on a path where half of you doesn't think it makes a bit of sense, but the other half knows your life won't make any sense unless you participate in certain activities that automatically draw out your passion for life.

You'll also find that the bigger the calling, the more likely it is that it will fling opposing energies into your life. For example, one part of you will want to awaken, while another part wants you to stay in the comfortable, safe but unfulfilling lifestyle. So what is *your* calling? What feelings come to you as you imagine fully with all of your senses, living your life with passion and purpose?

How do we know what our passions are? How do we uncover what brings us to a greater understanding of what our purpose is? And once we know our passion and purpose, how do we express them in a work environment so that our life is continually being fulfilled?

This chapter will lead you down a path of self-discovery through exercises and questions to reflect upon your own personal definition of your passion and purpose in life and in work. What is required is an open mind, a willingness to explore, and setting time aside regularly to reflect on the questions provided here. A growing intuition also will inherently bring wisdom to guide you toward making more gratifying career choices.

As we listen more to our intuition, we come into conflict with the status quo and others' expectations of who we are and what we should be doing. A natural consequence of aligning our own values and integrity is that we will inconvenience someone, including ourselves!

Creating a life of your own design, based on your known passion and sense of purpose, takes boldness, but the rewards of greater self-pride and just plain delight are worth it! Many of us have lost sight of our dreams, ideals, talents and passions in order to stay in survival mode, to support a family, or to live up to others' expectations . This path has led us to feel restless and unsatisfied, even though perhaps all our material needs are taken care of.

You can expect life to get a little bit crazy as you explore and play with new beliefs, concepts and connections to form your new life based on your own values, passions and personal definition of your life's purpose. It will take courage and determination to answer the questions honestly in this chapter. So, as you take this journey of self-exploration, now and throughout your life, it will be easier with a circle of supportive friends as you let go of what no longer serves you. Few people have uncovered their passion and purpose by themselves. As you follow your intuition or inner guidance, you will be able to engage more fully in your own life from a place of true strength, and at the same time support others as they strive to do the same.

A Wake-Up Call to Meaningful Work

Within the past decade or two, people have been talking about "worthy work." People don't just want a paycheck anymore; they want more than that. In *Zen and the Art of Making a Living*, Laurence Boldt writes about three alarm clocks in relation to waking up to our life's work.

First, there is your internal clock, the desire for creative self-expression. This alarm goes off when you feel stuck, stifled or bored in your current work situation. You have talents and abilities that are not being fully used in your job.. Maybe they're even being fully ignored! You go to work because you have to, not because you want to. When the internal alarm goes off, you think, "OK, I have to start moving on and doing something else. What are my passions? I have to find my purpose."

The second alarm clock is the external alarm which is a call to service, a call to a more meaningful experience of work. You become aware of what's happening in the world around you and you think about where you want to devote your attention. It could be the old call of the suffering of others or something else saying, "There's more out there for me to discover and to learn about."

The third clock is called the snooze alarm, because it wakes you up to the reality that the workplace is changing. Globalization, mergers and the electronic revolution have made work less labor-intensive, where fewer blue-collar workers are needed. Mass retail stores are putting some of the smaller stores out of business. You may think your job is secure but you never know for sure if you will be with a certain company or industry for any length of time due to the current economic situation.

If you do not pay attention to this internal alarm clock going off, if you ignore it, it may affect not only your work relationship but also your physical health or your spiritual/emotional well-being. The research on this is really shifting now. Experts used to say, "If you are in a stressful situation at work, it may affect your work." Now it is widely documented that stress not only will affect your *work* performance, but your health and emotional state, too .

You can choose to ignore it but if you want to move forward with your life, you really have to think about doing something about it. You have to ask, "What is it that I really want to do?" and "How can I do this in the world?" If you're stressing out over people and situations that you absolutely believe you have no control over, it is time for an emotional adjustment either by shifting your attitude or shifting into a more satisfying work experience.

So as we begin this undertaking it would be good to journal, to record your reflections during the periods when you are able to sit down and spend time in self-exploration and self-discovery about how you want your passions to support your purpose.

First of all, do something nice for yourself in terms of self-care. Too often we do so many things for others and get so involved in our really busy lives that we neglect ourselves. If you have been multitasking—doing a variety of things at the same time—you may be producing a lot of stress. Slow down. Stop. Give yourself time to pull yourself back and say, "Okay, all this is going on, but where am I? Who am I? Where do I want to go? Who do I want to be?"

Next, take a look at where you are now with regard to your "zest" for life. When you are engaged in expressing your passion and purpose, you will automatically experience vitality.

So reflect on the questions below and rate yourself according to how alive you feel now.

1. Do you feel a sense of balance between work, family and play?
2. Do you regularly laugh wholeheartedly?
3. Do you practice following your dreams?
4. Do you take time to meditate, reflect, journal?
5. Do you have emotionally healthy people in your life?

6. Do you feel enlivened through regular exercise?
7. Do you have a fulfilling spiritual practice?
8. Do you feel that you and others appreciate you, your life?
9. Does your recreation time re-set your stress levels?
10. Are you able to say "no" to situations and people that would cause imbalance to your life?

How many of these questions did you answer yes to?

Now that you have a sense of your abundance or lack of passion or aliveness in your life, the next step is to build a foundation to increase your sense of aliveness and at the same time acknowledge what people, situations or attitudes are robbing you of your feelings of passion and purpose.

Following is a list of some blocks to your "aliveness." Note the ones that you realize are keeping you from fully participating in life and add your own if not listed here.

1. Depression
2. External stressors (jobs, relationships)
3. Personal and others' unrealistic expectations
4. Procrastination
5. Vagueness about your personal goals or vision
6. Perfectionism
7. Lack of awareness of what you need to be satisfied
8. Overachievement/over-accommodation
9. Inability to express emotions freely
10. Laziness or underachievement
11. Chronic worrying
12. Overly analytical
13. Indecision
14. Fear of success

15. Fear of failure
16. Fear of change, taking risks, being vulnerable
17. Fear of letting others down

So now that you have a greater awareness of what keeps you from being more in touch with your passions and life's purpose, it's time to set some goals focused on gaining more control over these blocks.. Start by reflecting on when, where and with whom these energy zappers (emotional blockages) surface in your life. Be as specific as possible.

Then try to catch yourself at the onset of a blockage, thus increasing your self-awareness in the moment. Find a healthier replacement for behaviors, friends or situations that drain your energy. Be aware of your fears around change and note your successes and struggles with this process. Share with trusted friends or a counselor to keep you on track.

Below are some strategies to embrace which, once adopted, should start you on the path to leading a life with more passion and aliveness. Tailor the suggestions to your own emerging lifestyle. Stay open and challenge yourself to go beyond the familiar and into the unknown. Many rewards and gifts await you!

The Wheel of Life

The Wheel of Life exercise will help you learn where your level of satisfaction is with each area of your life and where more attention is needed to create a more harmonious balance. Within each spoke, indicate the percentage of your current satisfaction with the various areas of your life; for example, Family=65%, Wisdom=80%. You determine the definitions of each spoke name and the parameters for your percentages. Then consider how you might adjust a particular spoke of the wheel to bring more fulfillment and more balance into your personal and professional life.

An overabundance or a deficiency in one area can affect other components (e.g., overwork in your career can cause physical exhaustion leading to illness, stress resulting in emotional upsets affecting social relationships, and mental inefficiencies impacting decision-making).

Physical fitness has a major impact on your overall wellness. Employers also benefit through decreased medical costs and improved productivity on the job, two important considerations when more work is spread over fewer people. During the past two years, how many days were you off work or school due to medical reasons? Can you, or do you want to, offer a potential employer the advantages that go with a healthy lifestyle? What changes, if any, need to be implemented to increase your stamina and endurance?

THE WHEEL OF LIFE

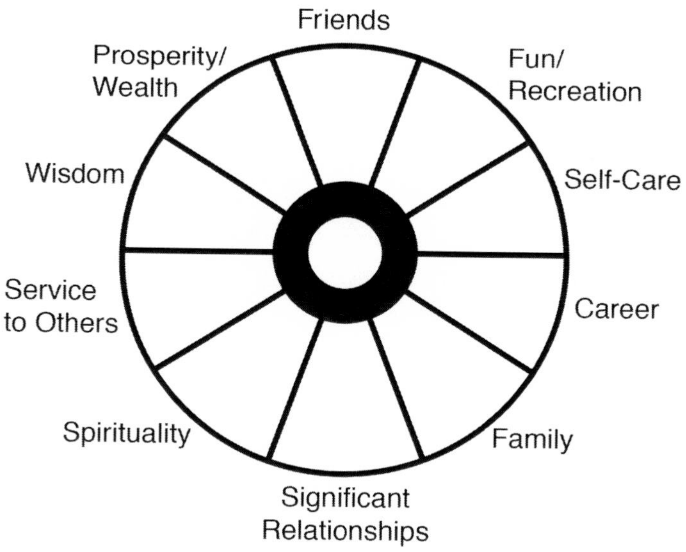

1. Discover where the areas in your life are in balance and where more attention is needed to create a harmonious balance.
2. Now prioritize the areas that you would like to bring more attention to and create strategies or goals to promote a successful resolution to the stress or lack of satisfaction currently experienced in these areas of your life.

3. Create a detailed vision of how you would like your life to unfold. This dream or ideal will be a navigational tool to determine if your action steps are bringing you closer to this vision. Make sure that your goals are SMART goals: Specific, Measurable, Achievable, Realistic and Timely. Set start dates and target dates for each goal and determine what action steps need to be taken as part of your strategy to achieve these goals.
4. Write down action steps that will foster more positive growth, such as remembering to laugh and smile more, volunteering for a charity that you value, being around supportive company, reading books about self-awareness, spending time in play and adventure, composing a daily gratitude list, affirming yourself and your efforts, increasing time for spiritual practices, de-cluttering your environment, carrying out the actions and letting go of attachments to the results.

Finding Your Purpose

Before we begin using exercises and questions to uncover your purpose, we will explore some basic myths that can block you from going forward and following your passion and purpose. You may think that only those who are extremely intelligent, determined or gifted will find their passion and purpose, but the truth is that *everyone*, including you, has a unique set of passions to support their life purpose and the full expression of that life purpose.

Myth # 1*: Discovering purpose is a task available only to those who have the luxury of time and circumstances to explore.* In reality, anyone who chooses to take the time to become more conscious of a life purpose is making the commitment to pursue this extremely fundamental right.

Myth #2: *Purpose relates only to those who are famous or fortunate with a big vision to serve many.* In reality, finding one's purpose is about finding your true self and expressing fully who you are. Everyone's purpose is uniquely his or hers. And it does not have to be on a grand scale.

Myth #3: *When the timing is right, your life purpose will be revealed to you.* Actually, most people start finding their purpose when they start asking the question of what life is all about.

Some people are gifted with this answer early in life but the majority of us have to consciously uncover their life's passions and purpose. Out of fear, some people "inherit" a purpose based on what their family expected of them or by following in their parents' vocational footsteps. These influences of family, friends, cultures, religions, or economic growth can overshadow the need to claim our own conscious choices. You do need to learn to listen to and courageously honor your own inner voice that leads to conscious decision-making about what you choose to manifest in your life.

How do you know whether you are unconsciously being influenced by others, rather than listening to your own inner voice when it comes to fulfilling your purpose? Here are some clues: Do you work just for the money? Do you stay in a job that you don't enjoy? Have you stopped learning? Have you stopped having confidence in yourself and your choices? Do you like who you have become? Do you feel you are powerless to change your circumstances?

Many people hold excuses up to prevent further exploration in discovering their life passions and purposes. Some of these excuses come in the form of beliefs, such as: I'm too poor, too young, too old, unhappy, don't have good health, am a member of a minority, am only one person, not educated, not free and independent. These realities can be viewed as challenges to be overcome in the pursuit of living your life's purpose.

Once you have an increased awareness of what passion means to you personally, how do you find purpose-filled work that will foster or reflect your passions? Defining your life's purpose allows you to connect who you are with what you do in the world, especially in the area of work. Write a statement of two or three sentences that states your personal vision of your purpose. Here are some questions to think about and ask yourself to help you further discover your life's purpose.

1. What activity was I doing the last time I lost track of time?
2. What issues or causes are important to me?
3. Do I have a healthy assessment of myself, my abilities, my dreams?
4. What do I like to do in my spare time?
5. What part of my current job or life activities do I thoroughly enjoy?
6. How do I want to be remembered?
7. What would I do if I could not fail?

It's really important to give yourself time to reflect on these questions. Enjoy the process of allowing yourself to acknowledge what you really love to do!

After answering the questions above, write down in your journal:

My life's purpose is to ...(for example, make the world a more beautiful place, help the disadvantaged find their voice, feed the poor, etc.) through ... (volunteering at a library, joining a social cause, or working in a company that values authentic communication, etc.) Defining your life's purpose is the first and most important step toward doing work you love based on your passions. Initially you may experience some subconscious resistance as you attempt to manifest your "dream job" based on your purpose, but there is probably less stopping you from going after the career you really want than you currently believe.

Perhaps finding work you are passionate about may mean you will need to change jobs. Or you may decide to start your own business. On the other hand, you may find a way to shift your perspective at your current job.

Visualization is an extremely effective way for you to create a new life for yourself. The key is to gain clarity on what you want and what is truly important to you.

Here are some additional questions you can ask yourself to see if patterns begin to emerge concerning your interests and passions. Consider whether you would like to use any of these interests in a work setting:

1. What do you feel so strongly about that you would devote time and effort to it?
2. List hobbies or activities you pursue in a typical week.
3. What magazines and book subjects do you pick up and browse through?
4. What organizations would you volunteer your time or your money to?
5. What general fields of study have you wanted to learn about?
6. What interests do your clothes reflect?
7. What do you daydream about?
8. Looking at snapshots you have taken, what interests do you see?
9. What classes have you taken in the last two years?
10. If you were asked to create a TV special, what would you do?

The Futures Letter

This exercise called "The Futures Letter" will help stimulate new ideas, inspirations and possibilities for creating a new and more satisfying future.

1. Pretend it is one year from now and you are writing a letter about your success. Share what has transpired and what you have accomplished during the past year, both career-wise and in your life in general.
2. The goal of this exercise is to identify your objectives for the next year. This format will help you connect with what you really want, not what you think you should do. While you no doubt know how to write about what is most compelling to you, addressing these important areas will make your insights more concrete:

a. What does your work life look like?

b. How do you feel about your work life?

c. What does your typical day look like?

d. Is there anything else that is important to you regarding your work/life?

Be sure to balance what you would love to happen in your life with what you believe can happen. So right now, begin working on your dream. Too many people resist doing this type of exercise because they make it more complex than it needs to be. It doesn't need to be perfect! In fact, perfection doesn't exist. This is a work-in-progress and always will be. Remember that the universe rewards focus, intent and action. Have fun!

Making Your Dream Real

Now take a look at what you are DOING to close the gap between your current work situation and your ideal workday. Here are a few examples of actions you can take now to clarify what your purpose is and how your work can reflect this back to you and others.

1. Contact people who are doing jobs that interest you and ask to do an "informational interview" with them to learn about their experience in the workplace. Just because a job or career sounds interesting to you doesn't mean that you would enjoy the daily realities entailed in that work. Informational interviews should be full of questions about work responsibilities, environment, teamwork issues, etc., but not about asking for employment. (More details about how to conduct an informational interview are covered in Chapter 7.)

2. Volunteer in an area where you could become a professional.

3. Take part-time work. Learn about the field without fully committing to long-term, full- time employment.

4. Take classes or training. There are a great number of cost-effective ways to learn more about a field, either through a one-day course or in-depth training.
5. Attend professional organizational meetings or conferences. This is a great way to meet others in the field who are excited about their work.
6. Know yourself. Through the exercises in this chapter and through other explorations, you will begin to discard the "shoulds" and live authentically, making right choices for great fulfillment. Ask yourself what you would do if you were financially independent and didn't have to earn money.

Most people who are combining passion and purpose in their life's work recognize that they are part of a bigger mission or cause than themselves. Ask yourself: "What are my talents and how can I share them with the world?"

Sometimes people have a satisfying job but find real purpose and passion in their hobbies and volunteer activities. The key: How can you increase your zest for life, your passions and live from your purpose as much as possible in the time you have been given.

Also, consider that if you do not enjoy your current job, it doesn't necessarily mean that you need to change vocations. It could be that you are working for the wrong company or the wrong people or that you are in the wrong position. You need to identify what you need more or less of to make your job situation more in alignment with your ideal work situation.

How do you know if you've found your purpose? It's a little like asking how do you know if you are in love with someone. You just know. When you find it, you'll know. Until then you will question and wonder and feel restless. So give yourself plenty of time to explore what your passions and purpose are. One of the best contributions you can make to humankind is to create a life that you find fulfilling and challenging and brings you joy. That's a great contribution to give to others.

Here is another story about owning our passions and purpose: Pat came to me in a distressed state of mind. He was a successful community developer with a Master's degree in urban planning. However, he was restless and kept thinking about his passion for historical preservation, which he never took seriously enough because he felt he couldn't make any money in that field and his parents would have been disappointed at his choice.

Instead, he took the safer route, but his subconscious had been tugging at him for many years. We talked about ways he could explore getting a certificate in historical preservation while working his job. He thought perhaps his current employer would let him take a leave of absence or reduce his work hours while he went back to school. With support and the willingness to live life honestly, most of us can find avenues that will open for us to follow our passions and enjoy living from purpose.

Now you might be saying, "Nobody will ever pay me for doing what I really love" or "I can't just get up and quit my job to do what I love." And there may be some truth in this. There are many factors to consider when making career changes, but I'll bet there are fewer obstacles than you think that are stopping you from going after the career you want.

You may not choose to change your career, so perhaps you will want to practice shifting toward a healthier attitude or perception in your current work situation. If you can learn to rate your level of enjoyment at work, or, actually, in any situation, and ask yourself how you can raise that number to a higher level of satisfaction, then you have a great tool to allow you better leverage and one that can bring more happiness into your life.

Finally, here are some questions for further reflection. Take a question a day and let the answer come to you over the course of your daily routines or simply sit and ponder one question at a time:

What if you tapped into your potential? What contribution would you make to this world? What if you stepped out and started pursuing your life passions or simply allowed yourself to explore the things that really feed you? How would your life be? How would you feel inside?

What if your pursuit of your passions didn't have to be all or nothing? What if you could define your involvement and create it in any way you chose? How would you feel inside?

What if you were truly fulfilled in every aspect of your life? How would you feel? How would you treat those around you? How would you treat yourself?

What if you were able to focus all your energy on the things that support, nourish and uplift you? How would your life change? How would you feel? What if you moved forward on those goals you've been procrastinating on for the past weeks, months or years? What if you allowed yourself to dream, to really want what you want for your life?

What if? It's your life. Are you ready to make it your best life ever?

Ann Ronan, founder of the Authentic Life Institute, shares these insights:

Uncovering Your Passions

OK, here's a secret. They're already there. You just need to acknowledge, embrace them and take action on them. So how do you uncover them?

Some of you may have had an "aha" or life changing moment that made you aware of a passion. Others discover their passions through intuition—an internal knowing that this is it. Others come to a gradual awareness through their experiences. Here are 3 methods to uncovering your unique passions.

1. *Think about the childhood activities you enjoyed. This is where the seeds of your passions lie. You were closer to your essential, true self as a child, before society, teachers and parents helped you forget what you truly love. I uncovered my passions through a combination of thinking about my favorite childhood activities and becoming aware of when I am happiest and "juiced" in the present.*
2. *Look at your current activities. When do you lose track of time? What topics do you naturally gravitate towards when you're reading a newspaper, browsing a bookstore, choosing movies? What are you*

doing when you get in the "flow" and lose all track of time? These are important clues to your passions.

3. *Imagine your ideal day. Take some time to write this down. Use all your senses. What are you doing when you wake up? What can you see and smell? How do you spend your time? What do you do for lunch? What kind of people are you working with? What kind of environment are you in—indoors, outdoors, traveling? How do you feel at the end of the workday?*

Action: Take 30 minutes to think about your childhood activities. Write down what you loved to do. How did you feel? What was it about the activity that excited you?

Then consider where you are today. What do you like about your current work? Dislike? What is pleasing to you in your living and work environments?

Ask others around you if they notice what it is you are doing or talking about when your face really lights up.

Finally take a peek into the future. If you could live an ideal life, what would it look like? Who is in it with you? Where do you live? What are you doing for a living?

As you come up with a list of potential passions, begin to experiment with them. Put your toe in the water by doing an activity related to your potential passion. Pay attention. What is it about the activity that excites you? Enjoy yourself as you uncover your passions!

Copyright © Ann Ronan, Ph.D. http://authenticlifeinstitute.com/?tag=ann-ronan

And finally, here is one of my favorite top ten lists from *Finding Your Perfect Work* by Paul & Sara Edwards.

Ten Different Ways to Do What You Love

Do what you love.

Provide a service to others who do what you love.

Teach others to do what you love.

Speak about what you love.

Create a product related to what you love.

Sell or broker what you love.

Promote what you love. Organize what you love.

Set up, repair, restore, fix or maintain what you love.

Find work, which you are passionate about, put passion into your work, and you will never work a day in your life!

- Kay Hirai

CHAPTER 4 : VERVE UP YOUR VALUES

All of us have values that, consciously or unconsciously, guide our choices and actions. Throughout our lifetime, some of our values may change depending on our age, our friends, work, hobbies, or other factors. Some values, however, have not changed and will not change, despite our exposure to diverse political, religious, and cultural influences. These are our core values and the ones we want to focus on here.

My favorite saying about core values is: "The degree to which we live our lives in alignment with our core values is the degree of fulfillment that we will experience." Core values reflect what is truly important to us as happy, healthy individuals. Core values relate to the heart of our being. They relate to the sacred essence of what we want to manifest in this world. When we honor our values regularly and consistently, life is good. When we are living from our core values, we feel fulfilled. Our values serve as a compass, pointing out what it means to be true to ourselves, and providing a sense of authenticity, self -respect and peace.

Many people cannot express what their five to ten core values are and thus are living lives unconnected to them. This ambivalence can lead to a life of unhappiness, discontent, conflict and unease. Some may feel conflicted because they are trying to live a life according to the values of a certain company, religious or political organization, or the values of their friends and colleagues or their partner rather, than living a life according to their own core values.

If you feel your life is unfulfilled and unhappy or has too much conflict in it, then it may be that you are leading a life that is not in accord with your own core values. The question is: Do you know your own personal core values? Do you know whether or not you are expressing them in your daily life?

Values Mining: The Jewels of Finding Fulfilling Work

Let's go jewel hunting for core values by considering the following question:

What in your life is important to you?

Step 1: Don't think about your answers at first. Just write down whatever comes into your head no matter how strange, amusing or worrisome it may seem. These first answers are probably your intuitive answers; sometimes those are closer to the truth than answers that you "think" about.

Step 2: Now think carefully about what is important in life for you. Take some time to consider your answers before writing them down in a word or short phrase. Don't worry if some of the same answers appear in your first list. Just write them down again.

Step 3: Now you have two lists. Go back and compare your two sets of answers to the question. Is there anything there that surprises you or concerns you? For example, if you are concerned because the word money is on your list, you might ask, "What does money mean for me?" Your answer might be "Money means security" or "Money means success" or "Money means freedom" or "Money means being able to provide for my family."

By answering the second question you can help uncover the real or underlying value for you. So for you, perhaps money is not the real value; perhaps the real value is "security" or "being successful" or "being independent" or "being able to provide for my family." It's always helpful to anchor or relate the values you express to real world situations. If you say you value "honesty" or "teamwork," write down what "honesty" or "teamwork" would mean in terms of your behavior and how it would impact others.

Exploring Your Peak Experiences

There are a number of other ways to approach uncovering your core values. One way is to ask yourself a number of questions about peak experiences you've had in your life. A peak experience can be defined as one that was especially full of feeling and where you felt alive and rewarded. Exploring your peak experiences can help you learn more about your values.

I also encourage you to look for the gap between the core values you listed and your current situation. This will allow you to find ways of acting that brings your behavior more in line with your values.

Digging Deeper

The following list of value-related words or phrases is provided for you to explore your values further. As you select words or phrases you are drawn to, you may combine two or three values that seem related as long as critical distinctions are not compromised or totally lost. For example, "Honesty/Integrity/Truthfulness" are closely related and can be considered together. "Honesty/Integrity/Freedom" combines concepts that are not closely related and combining them results in a loss of clarity. Remember, it is more powerful to relate the words you choose to a story about what you have or want to have in your life rather than simply picking words from the list.

Sample Values List

Humor	Productivity	Excellence
Romance	Orderliness	Success
No pretense	Participation	Expansion
Exhilaration	Sensuality	Harmony
Serenity	Intimacy	Authenticity
Contribution	Acknowledgement	Altruism
Integrity	Independence	Imagination
To be known	Vitality	Perseverance
Artistic	Transformation	Free spirit
Compassion	Goal oriented	Accuracy
Directness	Service	Performance
Recognition	Forward the action	Acceptance
Zest	Variety	Playfulness
Abundance	Inspiration	Lightness
Integration	Conformity	Joy
Community	Freedom to choose	Flexibility
Empowerment	Creativity	Personal growth
Risk taking	Elegance	Faith
Courage	Knowledge	Spirituality
Perfection	Ingenuity	Trust
Drama	Partnership	Bliss
Focus	Accomplishment	Wealth
Adventure	Tradition	Leadership
Collaboration	Stability	Adaptability
Completion	Persuasion	Curiosity
Sincerity	Personal power	Challenge
Self-expression	Honesty	Innovation
Peace	Growth	Clarity
Control	Dedication	Tenacity
Balance	Wholeness	Teamwork

More Tools for Discovering Your Core Values

Answering the following questions can help you gain more insight about your core values:

1. **Can you think of a time (at any age) when your life was especially full of feeling?** Perhaps there was an experience in your youth when something made you feel alive and rewarded, a time when you were very aware of the sweetness and goodness of life.
2. **What are your "must haves," the qualities you need in order for your life to be fulfilled?** What do you know that you cannot live without? For me, if I don't travel, something is missing in my life. I always find ways to bring it in. It might be in small trips but I love to travel. For example, if you love nature, maybe a small step toward honoring this value would be to take 20-minute walks in the park frequently.
3. **Can you think of a situation you handled in life where others said it couldn't be done and *you did it*?** What was it? How did you feel? How did you do it? There are values to be found in connection with that experience.
4. **Can you think of a defining moment in your life?** Completing the sentences below in your journal will help.

A defining moment was when….

What it taught me was ….

As a result you can count on me for …

One of my core values that I would like to continue to use for the rest of my life is ….

1. **Where have you taken your strongest stand?** What were you standing up for?
2. **In contrast, what drives you crazy?** What are you always complaining about? You are ultimately upset because someone or something is not valuing your values!
3. **And now imagine that you have passed away. Can you think of a statement or metaphor about your life?** What is the legacy you left behind? What do you want people to say about you?

From this list of questions you might discover ten values. Now prioritize those values. What are your top three values? Ask yourself how you are honoring them right now. If you aren't, then what are the next steps you can take to honor those values?

The steps can be small. If you are unable to express an important value in your work life, can you bring it into your personal life? For example, if you value adventure and your work environment doesn't offer adventure, make time to express it in your personal life. Now look at your three to five core values and ask yourself how you are honoring them on a scale of 1 to 10. If the score is below 8, there's something missing in your life.

Again, the degree to which you align your life with your values is the degree to which you're going to find fulfillment. So what can you do now, what small step can you take now to move your values up the fulfillment scale?

Knowing your values will help you make better decisions. If you have a major decision to make, ask yourself how you would be honoring your values when you consider the different possible choices to a given issue or situation. If you make a decision that is not reconfirming your values then it is likely that you will end up being an unhappy person .

By doing these simple exercises you are beginning to discover your personal core values. If your life is not exactly what you want it to be, you can make it so by first ensuring that you know and are fulfilling your core values.

Clarifying Your Work Values

Now that you know more about your fundamental core values, it's time to make an honest assessment of your work values. Below you will find three categories of values classified as intrinsic, extrinsic and lifestyle values.

Intrinsic Values are intangible rewards related to motivation and satisfaction at work. These are the values that make people say, "I love getting up and going to work." Some examples are:

- Enjoying variety and change at work
- Working on the leading edge
- Helping others
- Helping society
- Experiencing excitement
- Taking risks and physical challenges
- Feeling respected for your work
- Competing with others
- Having lots of public contact
- Influencing others
- Engaging in precise work
- Feeling a sense of achievement
- Expressing your creativity
- Working for a good cause

Extrinsic Values are tangible rewards or conditions you find at work including the physical setting, job titles, benefits, and earning potential. Extrinsic values often trap people into staying at jobs they don't like. They may find themselves saying, "I just can't give up my paycheck!" Other examples of these extrinsic values are:

- Having control, power and/or authority
- Traveling often
- Being rewarded monetarily
- Being an entrepreneur
- Working as a team

- Working in a fast-paced environment
- Having regular work hours
- Setting your own hours and having flexibility
- Being wealthy
- Having prestige or social status
- Having intellectual status
- Having recognition through awards/honors/bonuses
- Wearing a uniform
- Working in an aesthetically pleasing environment
- Working on the edge, in a high-risk environment

Lifestyle Values are personal values associated with how and where you want to live, how you choose to spend your leisure time, and how you feel about money. Some examples would be:

- Saving money
- Vacationing at expensive resorts
- Having access to educational or cultural opportunities
- Living close to sports or recreational facilities
- Being active in your community
- Entertaining at home
- Being involved in politics
- Living simply
- Spending time with family
- Living in a big city
- Living abroad
- Having time for spirituality or personal growth
- Being a homeowner

- Living in a rural setting
- Having fun in your life and at work

Step 1: Take a look at the values on each of the lists above and consider how important (on a scale of 1 to 5, 5 being most important) each of these values is to you.

Step 2: Rate the values in each list according to whether you always value, often value, seldom value or never value them. Check no more than 5 that you "always value."

Step 3: Next, determine which of the three categories (intrinsic, extrinsic, lifestyle) is most important to you. Consider how the values in each category are reflected in the work you currently do or in the position you would like to find. Look for overlap or values that seem to go together such as "Be wealthy" from Extrinsic Values and "Save money" from Lifestyle Values. If there is no overlap or compatibility between categories or if everything is important to you, prioritize your list by selecting your top ten values. Then narrow that list down to the five values you absolutely need both on and off the job.

Step 4: Once you have completed all three checklists (intrinsic values, extrinsic values, and lifestyle values), create a list of all the values you rated as 5s. If you have less than five, add the values you rated as 4s to the list. If your list of 4s and 5s has more than 20 values, you need to stop and prioritize your list. To prioritize, select no more than four or five values from each of these categories.

Step 5: Finally, write two or three sentences describing or summarizing how your values will apply to your ideal job. Knowing what's important will help you prepare for your next interview or help you find increased satisfaction with the job you have. In following this process, if you notice that what motivates you is already part of your lifestyle, it means you're living your values. Congratulations and enjoy!

The more you are actually enjoying the items you checked as "always value" in your current work situation, the more satisfied you will feel about your career life. Employing your work values is highly motivating for yourself as well as for the people with whom you work.

So what are your work values? If you're unhappy at work, it is likely because your values are not being met in the workplace. For example, if you value autonomy and independence and you have a boss who is constantly looking over your shoulder, you're not going to be happy there as the situation is totally opposed to who you are and what you value. The job may be fun, you may like the work, but you either need to change your job or change your boss or, possibly, adopt a reframing attitude to bridge the gap between your values and the way your supervisor and coworkers value you.

Your Work Environment

Ask yourself what work environment will give you a combination of the values that matter most to you. Once you have determined the top three to five values you hold important, brainstorm on your own or with friends and research which jobs would likely meet most of these values. Working with others on all stages of research and development is extremely helpful.

Work Values Inventory

Values are an important part in the career decision-making process. It is important to select career options that best fit your values. The following list will help you to identify those values that you think will be important to you in your work. Your work values may change as work situations change. It is important to evaluate your work values often. Write the following values in your journal. Read each one and decide if it is *always important* to you, *sort of important*, or *not important*. Place an "X" in the appropriate box. If your definition is different, use your own definition when rating the value.

1. My core values that are important to me in my life are:	Always important	Somewhat important	Not important
Achievement: Being able to meet my goals			
Balance: Time for family, work and play			
Independence: Control of my own destiny			
Influence: Able to have an impact on others			
Integrity: Standing up for my beliefs			
Honesty: Telling the truth and knowing others are telling the truth			
Power: Control over others			
Respect: Care and trust of self and others			
Spirituality: Believing in my core beliefs			
Status: Having influence and power over others			

2. I value work environments that are:	Always important	Somewhat important	Not important
Fast-Paced: Many things happening at one time			
Flexible: Work that is not set to a specific time schedule			
High Earnings: Work that has the potential to make a lot of money			
Learning: Work that is intellectually challenging			
Location: Work that is in a convenient place and an easy commute			
Predictable: Knowing what will happen each day			
Quiet: Work where there are few disruptions throughout the day			
Relaxed: Few pressures to get things done			
Structured: Work that is organized and has a specific set time			
Time Freedom: Work where I set my own schedule and plan how and when I do my work			

3. I value interactions with coworkers who are supportive:	Always important	Somewhat important	Not important
Competition: Work where I compete with others			
Diversity: Work where there are people with different ethnic backgrounds			
Friendships: Work where I can socialize with my coworkers			
Leadership: Work where there are good leaders managing the organization			
Management: Work where there is strong management			
Open Communication: Work where information is not held back from employees			
Recognition: Work where I am acknowledged for my work and contributions			
Support: Work where we help and support each other			
Teamwork: Work where working together is important			
Trust: Work where we can count on each other			

4. I value work activities that are:	Always important	Somewhat important	Not important
Analytical: Work that requires interpretation of data and information			
Challenging: Work that is mentally or physically challenging			
Creative: Work that uses imagination and creative talents to produce results			
Helping: Work that helps people			
Leading Edge: Work that creates new and innovative products or projects			
Physical: Work that has a lot of physical activity			
Public Contact: Work that has daily interaction with the public			
Research: Work that searches for new information			
Risk-Taking: Work that may be dangerous or risky			

YOUR WORK VALUES PROFILE

Review the "Always Important" values and choose your top five values. Write the values on the lines below with the most important value first. Check the line which indicates the section the value is from.

My Top 5 "Always Important" Values:

1. ______________________________

2. ______________________________

3. ______________________________

4. ______________________________

5. ______________________________

YOUR WORK VALUES STORY

Write a paragraph describing how you see your top 5 values in your current or future work.

____

____

____

____

____

____

____

Adapted from Work Values Inventory - Santa Cruz County ROP

The *Occupational Outlook Handbook* published by the U.S. Department of Labor is one good source of job descriptions. It provides information about what people do on various jobs, what the pay scale is, what the labor market is, and what are the demands of skills for the job requirements. Another way to learn more about jobs that interest you is to contact people who are doing those jobs and ask to do an "informational interview" with them to learn about their experience in the workplace.

After you've done your research (web-based search, informational interviews, etc.), you will be much closer to finding the right work situation that aligns with most of your values. Believe me, you will be much happier in a workplace that reflects those values. How you actually bridge this gap will determine how happy you will be in your work environment. You might ask, "What can I do now to make my work more compelling and expressive of my values for more moments or hours in the day?" A change of attitude, a change of job responsibilities, a change of immediate managers, or even a change of career, are some of the options available to you.

A clear understanding of your core values as well as your intrinsic and extrinsic work values and your lifestyle value are essential to living a fulfilling life. The more you can do to align your day with your core and work values, the happier you will be.

CHAPTER 5 : SUMMON YOUR STRENGTHS AND SKILLS

Recognizing Your Strengths

In order to find out what will make you happy at work or in your time away from work, you need to discover your talents and your strengths. People sometimes confuse strengths with skills. The basic difference is that skills are learned. You learn how to drive. Driving is a skill while your strengths or talents are innate, natural abilities. You may find you have natural talents in many different areas. When you see a little kid creating an amazing drawing or painting you say, "That kid is a natural." It's automatic. The child knows how to do it.

Take my son, for example. He has natural talent for using the computer. It's a gift of his. He taught himself desktop publishing because he was interested in it. He wanted to learn it. But he didn't go to school for it. He got on and he played and he played and he played and now he can do all kinds of stuff with desktop publishing. He didn't actually have formal training. Skills can help you perfect a talent and make it better. Developing skills can help you find your personal style. If you're an artist, you may have a natural gift or strength for drawing or painting but you still need to learn technique.

That is really the difference between skills and strengths. You can use skills to enhance your talents and strengths. When you are at work, you want to combine all your talents, all your strengths, and all your skills. Generally, when we first talk about talents, you find your talents and strengths in things that you love to do. So what you need to do is to look at the tasks you do. Identify the tasks that you absolutely love.

Someone said—and I love this quote--"A talent or strength is a present or gift that we have been given by Nature." It's a natural ability. We do not have to think about it. It's there in us already. Just think about this: Some people are naturally talented at sports. You've got recruiters going to all these high schools. What they're looking for is someone who has natural talent. Talent is like an innate ability. It is just part of who you are. Sometimes you may not even realize that you have it. Sometimes talents can be hidden. So if you want to look for talents, you first have to look at what you enjoy. What do you enjoy doing? What do you enjoy thinking about? What do you enjoy learning about? And what do you enjoy as a process?

Talents and strengths are related; they work together. An example of a talent could be the ability to organize people, to motivate people. There are people who are linguists. They don't have to work too hard at learning a new language. They just pick up a language naturally. You can learn a language, yes, and it is a skill, but some people have what we call natural ability. Some people pick it up one, two, three and others just struggle. It's a natural ability to be a linguist, to learn languages. For some people it just comes and it flows. So that is basically how you can recognize a talent.

I'm going to give you five questions to think about when you want to uncover your talents. It's basically tapping into what you enjoy. First of all, you want to think about what you enjoy most about your current work. Now, even if you dislike most of your work there may be one feature about it that you enjoy. So what is it that you enjoy most about your current work? Find that part of the job that you really love to do and do more of it. You can always re-craft your job to make it more interesting to you, to find the things that you really want to do more of. You can negotiate with your bosses, your management. Take on extra projects to do what you really love. Then at least you'll have more satisfaction at what you do.

Second: What do you most enjoy doing when you're *not* working? List your hobbies or your recreational interests.

Third: What do you enjoy most learning about? Believe it or not, we like to learn about things we feel we're good at—things for which we have a natural talent. It all flows together.

Fourth: What do you most enjoy making? It doesn't have to be a piece of art. It could be a project you've taken on.

Lastly: If you were financially independent and money was not a factor, what kind of work would you do?

These are just some questions that give you an idea of how to tap into your talents. Once you get a list of activities you enjoy, take the top 10, then ask three or four of your friends, "This is what I think I am really good at, what's your opinion?" See if you rated yourself correctly. Your friends may come up with something you hadn't originally considered to be a talent.

You may find that you feel a lot of resistance, confusion and fear when you ask yourself these questions. People need to stretch out of their "comfort zones." It's easy to be complacent. Some people find that they love to paint but only do it for personal satisfaction. Others who are passionate about their art are reluctant to offer it for sale for fear no one would buy it.

There is a classic book about this issue called *Do What You Love and the Money Will Follow,* by Marsha Sinetar. Basically, the author's message is that if you really follow your heart, if you really follow your passions, if you really use all your skills and strengths, you can make money. You really need to be using your strengths and talents to the full extent that you can every day at your work and during your recreational time. If you do that, you truly will be happy. It's almost guaranteed. If you are constantly tapping into and focusing on your strengths and talents, there is no question you're going to experience greater satisfaction, greater happiness in your daily life.

What Are Your Dependable Strengths?

Next, I want to share with you the process of finding your dependable strengths. This is a concept created by Bernard Haldane. I call him the grandfather of career counseling. He created the Dependable Strengths Institute. Finding your dependable strengths is a very powerful process.

The first step you have to take is to identify your life's good experiences, because your dependable strengths will emerge through these experiences. So how do you define a good experience? Ask yourself what you have done well, what have you enjoyed doing, and what were you proud of? These are the essential ingredients in a good experience. You did it well, you enjoyed it, and you were proud of it. Go back to your childhood and think of a good experience you had before the age of 10. It is surprising how our talents and strengths start appearing at an early age and they carry through with us the rest of our lives.

For example, I remember being in a school play when I was about eight years old. It was *Cinderella* and I was the prince's mother. Okay, here I was on stage and all dressed up and I had to get out in front of an audience. I still remember my lines. It was my first experience of being on stage. I said, "I love this, I love being in front of people." Even though my life's work was not to be in acting, I still love being in front of people.

So you look at a good experience you had before the age of 10 and then you can take it further. You come back to the present and you think, "What's a good experience I have had in the last three to five years?" It could be work-related but it doesn't have to be. What you need to do is come up with at least five good experiences because from there you're going to pull out what your strengths are. It's just amazing how powerful this is. Take this list of five good experiences and share it with some friends. Then write down all the strengths, all the talents, all the skills that you had to utilize to make this experience happen. Then ask yourself what you did in order to have that experience. What did you need to do? How did you prepare? What were the different steps along the way?

What I love about the concept of dependable strengths is that it really comes from inside you as a remembrance of a good experience. Once you have considered these five good experiences, you go through them and you look at "What are my dependable strengths?" The criterion is that a dependable strength shows up in at least three of your five good experiences. That's one of the keys. The other key is that you enjoyed it. It's so important—enjoy, enjoy, enjoy. You have to enjoy the experience. You may have skills and strengths that you don't enjoy. We all have skills that we use but we don't particularly like using them. These are not dependable strengths. Be glad you have them and can use them to serve you, but again, they are not your dependable strengths.

You want to use your dependable strengths as much as possible on the job. Knowing your dependable strengths will actually give you greater employability. It will give you renewed motivation. It's like finding and growing your best self. The process is really powerful because you tell other people what your good experiences have been and they're going to feed back to you descriptions and qualities of your strengths and skills and talents. Look for a pattern of experiences that you've had throughout your entire life. Of course you have to enjoy them. And of course, you must use it in the future to feel satisfied and happy. That's really the fundamental principle. The ideal is to really focus on your strengths to the fullest.

In the workplace, we are often assigned tasks we don't like and are not good at. We'll probably do the task or project with a lack of zeal. But it's not what we love. If possible, it is really better to give it to someone who enjoys doing it. This is a mistake that a lot of employers make, particularly on teams. They give people tasks they don't like to do and guess what? They don't get done very well. Part of the concept of dependable strengths is that if you know what they are you can say, "Well, I can do this." One of the last pieces of working with dependable strengths is using your strengths in working with others. It's great when people do a project together and say, "I will do this because I'm really good at it and I love it." Imagine you have a team and everybody on it is doing what they love to do. I mean, imagine the power of that? It's just fantastic.

Sometimes employers make mistakes when they assign a team project or promote someone who is good at his or her job. A company I won't name (but a major aircraft company in the Pacific Northwest) very often rewards good people and good workers. What do they do? They give them a promotion. Sounds like a great deed, right? Problem is that sometimes people who are great engineers end up being promoted to manager and hate it! They're just not good at managing others. They don't know how to do it. They get burned out. They get stressed because it's not a job they love. What they *do* love is engineering!

Another example is from a major computer software company—same thing. I know personally someone who was a technical writer. She loved technical writing. She was really, really good at it. What did they do? They appointed her manager. She quit after one year because she hated it. This is a mistake employers sometimes make, even when they're trying to reward someone for good work. Let people do what they love. This is the basic rule.

Bernard Haldane stresses that the more you know about your strengths, the more you will understand how to adapt to the changing demands of the workforce. Haldane recommends the following four basic steps to exploring your strengths:

1. Accept yourself as having a unique kind of excellence that is always growing within you.
2. Recognize that the elements of your excellence have been demonstrated from time to time throughout your life. These elements have most likely been demonstrated in good experiences you have made for yourself. Remember that "Good Experiences" in this case are defined as things you feel you did well, you enjoyed doing them, and you were proud of what you did.
3. Believe that by carefully identifying and studying your good experiences, you will find the pattern of skills and talents you have repeatedly used to make those experiences happen.

4. Focus on using this pattern of skills and strengths. They are reliable elements of your special excellence. These patterns of strengths provide clues to the kinds of career activities that are likely to be part of your future achievements regardless of your job titles or job descriptions.

Haldane offers five questions to ask yourself in identifying the Top Ten Good Experiences that will assist you in identifying patterns of strengths. Write your answers in your journal.

1. What is the good experience that first comes to your mind? Describe it briefly in your journal. What did you do to make it happen and what strengths did you use?
2. What activities give you the most enjoyment? These could include hobbies, volunteer work, ventures, family projects, work, school, or anything else. Give two or more examples.
3. In your last assignment, activity or work, which parts of it did you do best and enjoy most? Give two or more examples.
4. After completing your formal schooling, which two or three subjects did/will you continue to study and enjoy most?
5. In your journal, list up to ten (10) good experiences (see definition above) from any time of your life and any part of your life. Consider what you did to make them happen and what strengths you used.

Working within your areas of dependable strengths can only increase your potential and career satisfaction.

What Are Your Signature Strengths?

There are other kinds of strengths called "signature strengths," a concept which is based on the VIA (Values in Action) Inventory of Strengths put together by Martin Seligman and Christopher Peterson in their book *Character Strengths and Virtues.* I encourage you to go to Martin Seligman's website www.authentichappiness.com. The website has lots of free assessments on your signature strengths and your happiness quotient. It's absolutely amazing. You can analyze yourself just by going through the website. You can actually take a little assessment on your signature strengths. These are what we call "intrinsic qualities" that you can tap into at the workplace. That's the primary idea because if you're not using your strengths in your work, in your life, you will be unhappy. The secret of happiness is to use your strengths to the absolute utmost every day.

Below is a checklist of personal strengths that make a critical difference in various types of jobs. Read each word and select the ones you feel are most highly descriptive of you. Then think about how you can incorporate these strengths into your work or personal life and make a concerted effort to use them every day.

Personal Strengths Inventory

Academic	Democratic	Kind	Robust
Accurate	Dependable	Leisurely	Strong
Active	Determined	Light-hearted	Self-confident
Adaptable	Dignified	Likeable	Self-controlled
Adventurous	Dominant	Logical	Sensible
Affectionate	Easy-going	Loyal	Sensitive
Aggressive	Efficient	Mature	Serious
Alert	Emotional	Methodical	Sharp-witted
Ambitious	Energetic	Meticulous	Sincere
Artistic	Enterprising	Mild	Sociable
Assertive	Enthusiastic	Moderate	Spontaneous
Bold	Fair-minded	Modest	Spunky
Broadminded	Farsighted	Natural	Steady
Business-like	Firm	Obliging	Stable
Calm	Flexible	Open-minded	Tough
Capable	Forceful	Opportunistic	Trusting
Careful	Frank	Polite	Tactful
Cautious	Friendly	Poised	Tenacious
Charming	Generous	Practical	Thorough
Cheerful	Gentle	Progressive	Teachable
Clear-thinking	Good-natured	Purposeful	Tolerant
Cool	Healthy	Prudent	Unassuming
Clever	Helpful	Precise	Understanding
Competent	Honest	Quick	Unexcitable
Competitive	Humorous	Quiet	Uninhibited
Confident	Idealistic	Rational	Verbal
Conscientious	Imaginative	Realistic	Versatile
Conservative	Independent	Reasonable	Wholesome
Considerate	Individualistic	Reflective	Warm
Cooperative	Industrious	Relaxed	Wise
Courageous	Intellectual	Reliable	Witty
Curious	Ingenious	Reserved	Zany
Creative	Intelligent	Resourceful	
Daring	Informal	Responsible	
Deliberate	Inventive	Retiring	

Again, a major key to happiness is to use your strengths to the absolute utmost every day.

Analyzing Your Skills

When you are considering a new career, you will need to think about not only your signature and dependable strengths but also about the skills you have developed throughout your lifetime. A skill is something you can do, such as drawing, repairing, planning, organizing, or mediating. You may not be aware of your most vital skills. Often these are related to tasks you perform easily and well and simply take for granted. You may enjoy things like precision work, gardening or athletics and do them well, while other people may not do them well at all. Skills are basically divided into three categories. The categories are: self-management skills, transferable or functional skills, and job-related skills.

Self-Management Skills

Self-management skills are the day-to-day things we do to get along with others, to survive in this world. They're skills that make people unique: sincerity, reliability, tactfulness, patience, flexibility, drive, cooperation, persistence. Do not underestimate the importance of self-management skills in the job arena, especially ones that show motivation. For example, consider the ability to take initiative—employers love that. You might look at two employees and one just does what he's told but when he finishes his task he stops and says, "Duh…what do I do next?" The employee who has initiative will do their stuff and when they finish they'll move on to something else because they want to do more. That's a skill that's really valued by an employer. That's an example of what we call self-management skills. And employers do look for and value them. Very often they ask questions about these skills in interviews to really determine how a candidate will fit into their organization; that's what they want to know—how well you will fit into their team.

Transferable Skills

The second type of skill is what we call "transferable" or "functional." You can take these skills from one job to another. You can move from industry to industry, from career to career. What these skills say to an employer is "This person has done something similar and therefore can adapt." These are the skills that you use in an array of situations. They go across the board. They don't necessarily require training or background. Transferable skills are things like organizational ability or problem-solving.

Most of the skills you have can be done in a variety of situations and may be called by different names in different situations. These are called "transferable skills." Skills like planning, organizing, writing or selling are examples. It's important to consider the positions you have held and break down the tasks you have done to see which of the skills involved could be transferred to another type of work. If you've been a teacher, for example, and you want to do something outside the academic setting, you will want to think about other situations where you can use skills like counseling, communicating and motivating.

I used to work with welfare moms who never had paying jobs. They would come to me and say, "I have no skills. How can I get work? I have no skills." And I would say, "Oh really? Well, as a mom, tell me what you did." And they would say, "Well, you know, obviously I provided child care and I would clean, I would drive, I would organize the kids' programs, I would plan their vacations, I would teach them, I'd read to them, I would help them with their homework, I would give them advice if they asked me, I would solve problems. I would sometimes have to negotiate between them and their teachers, I'd have to make decisions. I'd have to manage the household, I would have to budget." And I would say, "Well, if those aren't skills, what are they?"

I want to say to all mothers, believe me, if you run a household, you have a multitude of skills that an employer will pay you for. So don't ever think that because you've never worked outside the home you have no skills. Absolutely not, that is a myth.

Job-Related Skills

The last category of skills is job-related skills. These skills are related to a specific occupation. For example, if you are an administrative assistant you may need to know about specific kinds of office machines. If you are a nurse you need to know how to give I-Vs. These are skills very specific to a job.

One thing you might notice though when considering the three different kinds of skills is that most job announcements are going to have just a few qualifications that are job-related and then all the other things they're asking for are transferable skills like organizational ability, problem-solving, or working with people. These are often the main skills that an employer considers important.

I want to recommend a great website that has a lot of really good exercises related to career change— www.nextsteps.org. One of the exercises I like best involves transferable skills. The site provides a whole list of transferable skills and asks you to consider which ones you have and which ones you don't have.

What Skills and Qualities Are Important to Employers?

According to the 2012 National Association of Colleges and Employers (NACE) Job Out/Oak Survey, the top 10 qualities/skills employers seek are these transferable skills:

1. Ability to work in a team structure
2. Ability to verbally communicate with persons inside and outside the organization
3. Ability to make decisions and solve problems
4. Ability to obtain and process information
5. Ability to plan, organize and prioritize work
6. Ability to analyze quantitative data
7. Technical knowledge related to the job

8. Proficiency with computer software programs
9. Ability to create and/or edit written reports
10. Ability to sell or influence others

It is interesting to note that without fail, communication skills and teamwork rank high on the list of skills employers want year after year. Which of the top 10 skills do you excel in? How have you demonstrated these? How can you develop them further?

Take Stock of Your Transferable Skills

Review the tasks in the following five categories and write in your journal all the skills you have. Then go back and circle the 10 skills you would enjoy using most. List these top 10 skills in your journal and write a brief example of how you have demonstrated each skill in a job, class, internship, or extracurricular activity. This will help as you consider career options and as you prepare for your job or internship search and interviews.

Design & Planning - *Imagining the future, developing a process for creating it*

anticipating problems, creating images, designing programs, displaying images, creating images, brainstorming new ideas, improvising, composing, thinking visually, anticipating consequences of action, conceptualizing

Communication - *Exchange, transmission and expression of knowledge and ideas*

speaking effectively, writing concisely, listening attentively, expressing ideas, facilitating discussion, providing appropriate feedback, negotiating, perceiving, nonverbal messages, persuading, describing feelings, interviewing, editing, summarizing, promoting, working in a team, making presentations , thinking on one's feet, dealing with the public

Organization, Management - *Directing and guiding a group in completing tasks and attaining goals*

initiating new ideas, making decisions, leading, solving problems meetings, deadlines, supervising, motivating, coordinating tasks, assuming responsibility, setting priorities, teaching, interpreting policy, mediating, recruiting, resolving conflict, organizing, determining policy, giving directions

Research & Planning - *The search for specific knowledge, setting goals*

analyzing ideas, analyzing data, defining needs, investigating, reading for information, gathering information, formulating hypotheses, calculating and comparing, developing theory, observing, identifying resources, outlining, creating ideas, identifying resources, critical thinking, predicting and forecasting, solving problems

Motivated and Unmotivated Skills

Bernard Haldane makes a distinction between what he calls "motivated skills" and "unmotivated skills." Motivated skills are things you like to do and do well. There may be other things that you do well but you don't like doing them. These are your unmotivated skills. For example, you may love to cook and cook well. This would be a motivated skill. You may also be good at cleaning up after cooking but you may not enjoy doing it. This would be an example of an unmotivated skill. In choosing a career you will want to be able to maximize opportunities to use your motivated skills and minimize the need to use your unmotivated skills.

We all have skills. Some we like and some we don't. And the skills we don't particularly like may be useful to us. For example, I can do basic word processing. I'm delighted I know how to do it, sure. But do I want to sit behind the computer all day? Absolutely not! So it's a skill that's useful to me but it's not one that I would put on my list of skills that I want to use on my job.

Every job asks you to do certain tasks. The tasks involve skills. So you want to find a job that is going to match the skills you enjoy using. In my case, for example, one of the accomplishments that I am most proud of is that before the age of 27, I traveled around the world by myself. It was a wonderful experience. I love to travel. It's one of my top values.

In thinking about my early travel experience, I asked myself, "Okay, what did I need to do in order to make this happen?" Well, I had to plan, I had to organize, I had to arrange. I had to budget. I had to be very flexible. I learned a lot about flexibility because although I had plans, sometimes they didn't work out. Of course I also had to be a really multicultural person and learn how to get along in a lot of cultures. I had my ears and eyes wide open to be able to pick up different little nuances of languages. There were a tremendous number of skills that I needed and they were all transferable. And they were skills that I enjoyed using.

The following Transferable Skills Checklist was compiled to help you identify transferable skills that you might otherwise overlook. Copy the checklist in your journal, adding any transferable skills you have that are not listed. Note how each skill applies to your situation.

- **Enjoy**– Note if you enjoy using this skill.
- **Do Well**–Note if you are particularly good at using this skill.
- **Must Use in Future Work**–Note if you actually want to use this skill in your work in the future.

Notice the "Key Skills" in the upper left column. These are the most important transferable skills. They are enthusiastically sought by employers and tend to result in more responsible positions and higher pay.

I really want to stress that, when you're looking to find a career that fits you, you need to look at *all* of your skills: your self-management skills, your transferable skills, and your job-related skills. Make a list of all of them and underline the ones that are your motivated skills. This is the critical factor. Look for work where you can use the skills you enjoy using.

Transferable Skills Checklist

KEY SKILLS

instructing others

managing money, budgets

managing people

meeting deadlines

meeting the public

negotiating

organizing/managing projects

public speaking

written communication skills

USING MY HANDS/DEALING WITH THINGS

assemble things

build things

construct/repair buildings

drive, operate vehicles

good with hands

observe/inspect

operating tools, machines

repair things

use complex equipment

DEALNG WITH DATA

analyze data

audit records

budgeting

calculate/compute

check for accuracy

classify things

compare

compile

count

detail-oriented

evaluate

investigate

keep financial records

locate answers, information

manage money

observe/inspect

record facts

research

synthesize

take inventory

WORKING WITH PEOPLE

administer

care for

confront others

counsel people

demonstrate

diplomatic

help others

insightful

instruct

interview people

kind

listen

mentoring

negotiate

outgoing

patient

persuade

pleasant

sensitive

sociable

supervise

supervise

tactful

teaching

tolerant

tough

trusting

understanding

USING WORDS, IDEAS

articulate

communicate verbally

correspond with others

create new ideas

design

edit

ingenious

inventive

library research

logical

public speaking

remembering information

write clearly

LEADERSHIP

arrange social functions

competitive

decisive

delegate

direct others

explain things to others

influence others

initiate new tasks

make decisions

manage or direct others

mediate problems

motivate people

negotiate agreements

planning

results-oriented

risk taker

run meetings

self-confident

self-motivated

solve problems

CREATIVE/ARTISTIC

artistic

drawing, art

expressive

perform, act

present artistic ideas

dance, body movement

OTHER SKILLS (Make a list)

The Final Ten

Once you've completed the checklist, go back over the list, review the skills you've checked and write in your journal the 10 that you feel most strongly about wanting to use in your future work.

Confidence and Fulfillment

The more you have a firm understanding of the skills you can bring to the workplace, the more confident you will be in setting out on your path to a new career. The clearer you are about the skills you truly enjoy using, the greater will be your chances of finding the career that is right for you.

CHAPTER 6 : DEVELOP DYNAMIC DECISION-MAKING STRATEGIES

Finding a career that's right for you is a process. As you know, we all change during our lifetime. What's right for us today may not be right for us in five years. People change careers in America generally between five and seven times in a lifetime. This is just something to bear in mind so you don't get caught up in the dead-end thinking of, "This is my choice and I have to stick with it for the rest of my life." You don't because you grow and as you grow you may change and you may find what was rewarding to you once may not be rewarding at a later time.

You have to embrace the change. But the career development process remains the same each time you make a change. The first question you need to answer is, "Who am I?" That's the bottom line. Then you have to know what your interests are and what you are passionate about. You need to explore your values and assess your skills, your strengths, and your talents.

Strategy for Decision-Making

There are action steps you can take to gather information about the world of work. You can do research in the library, you can attend workshops, or you can talk to people. Through books, the internet, and talking with people, you can find a description of the job you're interested in, how much it pays, and how the labor market is in that field.

It's very important to talk to people who are actually doing a job you're considering and to find out what the job is really like. We call these informational interviews. Most people are willing to be helpful if you say, "Hey, I'm going through a career change," or "I'm a student and I'm interested in this field. Could I meet with you for twenty minutes and ask you some questions?" Go to that person's office to see what it's like.. Find out as much as you can about the concrete details of the job before you make a decision to enter that career path.

Once you have gathered information about possible careers that align with your passions, your purpose, your values, your strengths and your skills, you will need to have an effective strategy for choosing among the alternatives.

We all have different decision-making strategies. Many of us learn from the bumpy road of life experiences. We try something and we say, "Oh. I don't like this." Okay, so you learn from that experience and you move on to something else. Below is a list of some of the decision-making strategies that you might follow. Look over the list and note in your journal the ones that you use most of the time or some of the time.

I usually make my decisions:

1. By choosing the alternative that would lead to the most desirable result, regardless of the risk involved. (Wish Strategy)
2. By choosing the alternative that is most likely to avoid the worst possible result. (Escape Strategy)
3. By choosing the alternative that is most likely to have the highest probability of success. (Safe Strategy)
4. By choosing the alternative that has both a high probability of success and one which I highly desire. (Combination Strategy)
5. By choosing with little thought or examination of the situation, i.e.., taking the first alternative. (Impulsive Strategy)
6. By choosing to let circumstances decide for me, i.e., leaving it up to fate. (Fatalistic Strategy)
7. By choosing to let someone else decide for me. (Compliance Strategy)
8. By choosing to postpone thought and action, i.e., "crossing the bridge when I get to it." (Delaying Strategy)

9. By choosing to collect too much data and to spend too much time analyzing alternatives. (Agonizing Strategy)
10. By choosing to make a mystical preconscious choice, i.e., "It feels right to me." (Intuitive Strategy)
11. By choosing to accept responsibility for the decision, but being unable to start the process. (Paralysis Strategy)
12. By choosing a process which ends in a satisfying result, i.e.., a rational approach with a balance between cognitive and affective factors. (Planning Strategy)

Obviously some strategies are more effective than others. Generally, the most effective decision-making strategies are those that are considered safe strategies. When you analyze your options carefully and then decide which is the better alternative, this is called a "safe strategy."

I like what I call a "combination strategy," which involves using your intuition along with your analytical powers. By all means use your intuition. If something feels good, go for it. But there is also an analytical component where you do your homework by going to the library and the internet and going on informational interviews and asking questions about aspects of the job that are important to know.

Even some of the strategies that are usually ineffective may be appropriate in certain situations. For example, the "delaying strategy" might be best if you really need more information and you have plenty of time to get it. Or if none of the available alternatives is very desirable you might take the "escape strategy" and choose the alternative that is most likely to avoid the worst possible result. And it could work. All decision-making strategies will work for you to some extent. But to make wise decisions you need to look at the combination of a little bit of this and a little bit of that, analyzing the options then feeling it intuitively and deciding what's best for you.

Decision-making is a process—a process that can be so short as to be almost instantaneous or one that can so completely involve your thoughts as to lead to paralysis. The process presented here will enable you to select the appropriate strategy for various situations.

1. The first step is to recognize that a decision is necessary. Understanding the need for a decision and the time of that decision is a vital part of the process. Must the decision be made immediately or can it be deferred while information is gathered and various options are defined and considered? Sometimes it is wiser to wait—sometimes it is wiser not to decide.
2. The second and very critical step is to define the situation. This involves defining the purpose for the decision and establishing the desired goal and objectives. Quite often, how you define the situation will automatically determine the decision that will be made.
3. The third step is to begin to gather information, both occupational and personal. During this phase, options begin to open up which in turn may require additional information. The two (information and options) are interrelated: one must continually be checked against the other.
4. As options are defined, possible or probable outcomes must be examined and weighed against your willingness and ability to take a risk. Deciding to make a change can be very threatening. Staying in a situation which is unsatisfying often is safer than risking the unknown. Your willingness to take a risk is directly related to the desirability of the outcome, which in turn is determined by knowing and understanding your values.
5. Each of the preceding steps has been an information-gathering and evaluation process. The next step is to make a final evaluation and to select the options to implement or pursue. At this point you should review each of the options for all of the factors that may apply and then select that which appears to be "best," the one that appears to result in the optimal outcome for you.

6. The next step requires that the decision be implemented. No decision has been made until it has been put into action.
7. Finally, you need to evaluate the success or progress of your action. If necessary, reconsider and re-enter the process. Nowhere is it written in stone that you can't change your mind! It is far better to change your mind than to stick with a decision that you know is wrong for you.

To summarize, here are the steps involved in decision-making:

1. Recognize the need for a decision.
2. Define the decision to be made.
3. Gather information and define your options.
4. Determine the probable outcomes and your willingness to take risks.
5. Evaluate your options and select one.
6. Take action to implement the option you have chosen.
7. Evaluate the outcome of your decision.

This process takes courage. What we're talking about is a leap of faith. Go through this process as many times as you need to in order to become clear on who you are, what you want, and what your interests, values, passions and purpose are. Then develop a strategy to test your choices for your next career path.

Setting S.M.A.R.T. Goals

Your chances of achieving success in carrying out the actions you choose will be greatly enhanced by your ability to effectively set goals that give order and direction to your efforts. Here are the qualities that need to be considered in effective goal-setting:

S – Specific. Your goals should be stated in detail, not in vague terms.

M – Measurable. Your goals should be stated in language that includes definite quantities so that the degree of your success can be evaluated.

A – Achievable. You need to be realistic about what you can actually do and avoid setting yourself up for failure

R – Relevant. Make sure that the goal aligns with the actual outcome you want to achieve.

T – Targeted. Give yourself a realistic, definite time frame for carrying out the action.

Take this opportunity to practice effective goal-setting by applying the above guidelines to a result that you want to achieve in your life. For example, suppose you want to reduce your current expenses in order to have more money to invest in the future. You might set a goal like, "I will reduce my monthly long-distance phone costs to $45/month over the next six months."

The more often you apply the guidelines of S.M.A.R.T goal-setting to results you want to achieve, the more you will become accustomed to doing it automatically. Whenever you think of a result that you want to achieve, you will begin to think of it in terms of goals that are specific, measureable, achievable, relevant and targeted.

Strategies for Achieving Your Goals:

- Commit yourself to setting goals.
- Write down your goals and objectives.
- Post copies of your goals where you can see them every day.
- Read your goals often.
- Practice visualizing yourself completing your goals. How will your life be different?
- Tell others about your goals.
- Reward yourself for completing activities and objectives leading to your goal.
- Believe in your ability to achieve your goal.

Motivation and Setting Goals

What would you like to accomplish at the end of one year? You can gain additional motivation for working on your current goals by considering what your lifetime goals are and relating them to your present life.

What Are Your Lifetime Goals?

Project yourself five years from now. What are your career goals? How old will you be? Where are you living? What is your family or marital status? What is your occupation? What is your salary? How did you accomplish this goal? What difficulties or setbacks did you encounter in working toward that goal? What kinds of things or people were most helpful to you in reaching this goal?

Now think about this coming year. What are your career goals? How will you accomplish these goals? What difficulties or setbacks might you encounter in working toward these goals? What are the things you need to do in order to accomplish this year's goals?

Now list the activities you will do this week and the things you will do today that relate to your goals for this year. You now have a "to do" list.

The S.W.O.T Exercise

The S.W.O.T. Exercise is a powerful tool that you can utilize in carrying forward the actions you choose to take as you pursue your career goals. S.W.O.T. stands for Strengths, Weaknesses, Opportunities and Threats. Try this exercise with one of the career options that aligns with your passions, values, strengths and skills.

Create the following S.W.O.T. diagram. Draw a large square. Divide it into four quadrants and label the four smaller squares. For easy comparison, put strengths next to weaknesses and opportunities next to threats. Write the words or phrases that apply to your situation in the appropriate boxes.

Strengths	**Weaknesses**
Opportunities	**Threats**

Source: www.Monster.com

Your strengths are your internal, controllable, positive attributes, such as relevant skills, competencies, work experience, education, network, and enthusiasm.

Your weaknesses are your internal, controllable, negative attributes, such as poor work habits, lack of work experience, lack of relevant education, no network, lack of direction, weak career management skills.

Opportunities are uncontrollable external events that you can use to your advantage. Examples would be favorable industry trends, a booming economy, specific job openings.

Threats are uncontrollable external factors that work against you such as industry restructuring, consolidation, changing market requirements, reduced demand for your skills.

Use the results of the S.W.O.T. Exercise to validate your current position, understand the skills, attributes and experiences you should emphasize when interviewing and know which ones to downplay. You can also use the exercise to determine possible career-planning action steps by: 1) strengthening a specific skill or adding something to your strengths quadrant; 2) minimizing or eliminating a weakness; 3) pursuing or exploiting an opportunity; and 4) protecting yourself from threats. You can revisit the S.W.O.T. Exercise each time you make a decision to take action on a step along your career path.

Likes and Dislikes

Here is another exercise to help you focus on the qualities you are seeking in setting goals for your future career moves. In your journal, list the past three jobs you have held. Under each job, write down the things you liked and disliked about each job. Review your entire list and circle the three characteristics you would like to be part of your next job. Then mark the three qualities/activities you would avoid in your next position.

This is also a good time to go back and review the "Futures Letter" that you wrote in Chapter 2. Notice whether your ideas about your career moves have changed and developed since you wrote that letter.

Choosing Well

Moving forward boldly with your decision-making process is essential to your success in your career and in all aspects of your life. Career coach Linda Markley (http://www.clovercoaching.com) notes, "Many people put off making choices either from a fear of making the wrong choice or simply not getting around to it. Paradoxically, not making choices is harder work in the long run. If we make the big choices about what we want in our lives we have a direction, a blueprint against which we usually make the small choices (like what to pay attention to, what to do next) more obvious."

Markley offers the following quiz to help evaluate just how effectively you are choosing:

1. Is there joy, lightness and ease in your life? Always? Often? Sometimes? Rarely? Never?
2. How often are you wholeheartedly involved in what you're doing?
3. How often do you feel good about what you are doing and who you are with at that time?

4. How often do you feel stress or strain?
5. How often are you bored?
6. How often do you regret having committed yourself yet continue anyway?
7. How often do you miss something important to you (like fun, time with loved ones, exercise, study, growing your business)?
8. How often do you consciously choose?
9. If you could do anything with or without anyone, how often would that coincide with what you do?
10. How much of your life is better than it was this time last year?
11. How much of your life will be better this time next year?

"People who choose well have more of what they want in their lives," says Markley. "Indecision is exhausting. Choice is freeing."

Stopping Analysis Paralysis

Celestine Chua, writer and founder of *Personal Excellence: Be Your Best Self, Live Your Best Life* (http://personalexcellence.co identifies indecision as "analysis paralysis," a state of over-thinking about a decision to the point where a choice never gets made, thereby creating a paralyzed state of inaction. She offers the following tips for this condition:

Tip #1. Differentiate Between Big and Small Decisions. Give a decision only the time and effort that it deserves based on its importance. If the decision isn't going to make any major difference to your life in a year's time and there are no serious consequences that will come out of it (e.g., picking a mismatched shade for your wedding table linen), then it is a small decision. Chill and let go. Spend as little time and effort as you can to nail it.

Tip #2. Identify Your Top Objective(s). Before entering into the decision-making process, identify your top objective(s) for this decision. Then use that to guide you in your decision-making. This will help you to arrive at a valid decision more quickly.

Tip #3. Perfection is not the key; "Moderately okay" is. Unless it's a life-altering decision, perfection isn't the key. Your role is to pick a moderately okay decision in a fair amount of time then move forward after that. Every option has its pros and cons and it's very hard to be in a situation where the perfect choice is available right there and right then. While you can work through and hunt down the perfect choice, it comes at a high cost. The 80/20 rule applies, where you need to invest 80% of effort just to achieve that incremental 20% improvement in your final decision.

Tip #4. Eliminate the Bad Options. Next, eliminate the bad options. Having a flood of options can clutter up the decision-making process so eliminate the bad ones right away to make it easier to assess. Refer to your objectives for making this decision (see Tip #2), identify the options that will definitely not meet your objectives and get rid of them. The ones that are left should be the considerably good ones which then allows you to make a more pinpointed assessment.

Tip #5. Pick One and Go—Don't Look Back After That. If you are stumped by the options and you are not sure which one to pick then just pick one and go. Don't look back after that. While this may seem reckless, it actually isn't. The reason why you have shortlisted these options is because they are reasonably good. If it's really crappy, you would have eliminated them as per Tip #4! Now no matter which option you pick you will miss out on the benefits exclusive to the other options since each option probably has its unique pros and cons.

Tip #6. Let Go of Your Childhood Stories Surrounding Decision-Making. If you constantly freeze in the face of decisions and your paralysis always seems to have a life of its own then it's possible that there's a childhood story driving you to act this way. What is your childhood story for decision-making? How can you let go of it?

Tip #7. Set a Hard Time Limit. A well-known rule known as Parkinson's Law says that "Work expands so as to fill the time available for its completion." This is the same in decision-making. When you don't set a time limit for your decisions, each decision can expand monstrously to take up your entire consciousness and schedule as you find new options to mull over, new details to analyze and every reason to contemplate the decision further and simply not commit to a decision. To solve this, set a hard time limit for your decision. Your time limit should be based on the importance of the decision.

Tip #8. Delegate the Decision to Someone Else. This tip is a little sneaky since you are effectively removing yourself from the decision-making process and shifting the decision-making responsibility to someone else. However it works if you trust the opinion of that person and you're okay with not handling the decision. Delegating doesn't have to mean hiring. You can also delegate personal decisions to your loved ones.

Tip #9. Get the Opinion of Someone You Trust and Go with It. This is slightly different from Tip #8 in that you still take ownership of the decision even though you're basing it on someone else's opinion. Get someone with insight in the area you are consulting on. If their recommendation makes sense go along with it; if not, pick the one you prefer. Either way, getting their opinion accelerates your decision-making process since you get more input to help you decide what you really want.

Tip #10. Channel Your Energy into Other Things. If you are still in analysis paralysis mode despite the nine tips, it's possible that you simply have extra energy that's not being channeled into more meaningful areas! Find more important tasks to devote yourself to. You'll be much more productive this way. You'll also find yourself getting clarity in your decision as you spend time away from it.

Maintaining Balance and Managing Overwhelm

Both during the job search process and on the job after you have achieved your goal and are doing work that is truly fulfilling for you, the following guidelines will help you keep perspective on your life:

1. First things first: Honoring the activities that give you resilience by practicing them daily. These activities could include: Taking time to exercise, meditating, eating well, and staying in contact with supportive people.

2. Everything is perfect: AND there is room for improvement. Learning to accept the way things are (You don't have to like it or want it) gives you a place to start.

3. Create accountability and celebrate success: Break down each project into tangible desired outcomes and deadlines. Be accountable to someone you trust. And then find appropriate ways to celebrate each milestone.

4. Perspective: There are many ways to look at a challenging situation. Realize that you will do your best with the given information at the time knowing that our understanding is continually maturing as we learn from each life experience.

5. Establish an orderly environment: When your insides are churning with anxiety over multiple commitments, create order outside. An orderly environment is calming.

6. Eliminate and delegate actions: Make a list of activities you could eliminate from your schedule or delegate them to someone else.

7. Be real: However linear or spontaneous you are, ground your choices in your real experience. It doesn't make sense to simply ignore a deadline or to pretend that a complex task can be done in ten minutes.

8. Design it and live it: Imagine and play with what your perfect week would be like. Write it down, schedule it on paper, and then begin to live it. What do you intend to create for yourself? Put this sheet where you see it daily.

9. Recognize the Gremlin: The Gremlin is the narrator in your head who constantly gives you negative messages about who you are, what you can and cannot do, the mistakes you are making—the list goes on. Learn to simply notice what messages are from him/her and then choose to ignore them. Perhaps easier said than done—but that's a subject for another book.

10. Breathe: First, last and always. Let a rising bubble of anxiety remind you to breathe deeply and center yourself.

It's your divine right to ask for what you want. And asking for a career that's right for you is no exception. We spend at least one-third of our lives working. That's quite a bit of our lifetime. And another third is sleeping. And the other third is the time we spend in other activities outside of work. So your work life is a big, big part of your life. You want to be doing something that you love and enjoy and are happy with. There's no question about it. It's really very important and knowing how to use the best decision-making strategy will help to ensure that you arrive at the place where you want to be.

CHAPTER 7: NOURISH YOUR NETWORK

The concept of networking is simple: It's letting people know that you're in the job market and telling them about your interests and the kind of work you are seeking. Networking is also about asking for advice and assistance in achieving your career objectives.

What networking does is to tap into the hidden job market. This market is approximately 80 percent of the jobs that are available every day and do not get advertised. It is a myth that all jobs are advertised. If you think about it from the perspective of most employers, when there is a job opening within their company what are they going to do first? They are not going to put an ad in the newspaper or list it on the internet unless they really have to because they will receive hundreds of applications. Instead, they will ask in-house to see if fellow workers have contacts that might be a good fit for the company. It is much easier to interview five people who have been referred through employees or friends of employees than to laboriously go through a hundred résumés. This is what the hidden job market is all about.

So how do you tap into this market?

A lot of it involves researching and contacting employers. It involves checking organizations, talking to people, writing letters, joining job-finding clubs, visiting job and career fairs. But the most important key is a referral by or through someone. The old adage is absolutely true: It is not *what* you know but *who* you know that matters.

Take my ESL students, for example. They're relatively new to America and when I ask them, "How did you find your last job?" two-thirds of them will say their brother or a friend had connections.

Talk to anyone you know and tell them, "I'm looking for work in this industry or region. Do you know anyone who can help me?" This is an example of the theory about six degrees of separation, which simply means there are six people between us and what we want and those people can help us get there. Names are magic. If you write, email or call about a job opening and say, "John Smith referred me," you will get more attention than if you make a random phone call. That's the key. So let's start learning the art of tapping into the hidden job market.

How does networking work? Everyone you know and everyone you meet or will meet is a contact and a potential resource of career guidance and referrals to important connections. First, make a list of everyone you know. Be sure to include the names of friends, friends of friends, parents and relatives, your children's friends or parents, classmates, teaching assistants, and professors. Add bosses and coworkers (past and present), and people you have met at the health club, while traveling, or doing volunteer work. Even include your list of professional contacts, like your doctors, insurance agents, bankers, accountants, etc. Expand your list with people from social, political, or religious organizations.

Here's just one example of how your network can serve you: In today's job market, many companies—particularly the larger ones—insist that you apply first online, and it often involves a lot more than emailing a résumé. Sometimes you need to complete an application online as well, and even fill out an assessment. It's like confronting a vast wasteland as you wonder, "Where does it go? Did they get it? What did they think? Will I ever hear back?" This is an occasion when utilizing your network can help. Let's say you're applying for a job at a hospital. Ask yourself, "Do I know anyone who works for this hospital? Is there anyone I know who knows someone who works there?" Spread your wings and ask around. Go to LinkedIn, Facebook, Twitter. See if you can find someone within the company who can help pull your application and/or résumé out of the pile and put in a good word for you. Names and contacts are still magical. They can help you get that job.

I have a friend who did exactly what I'm suggesting. She applied for a job at a shipping company in the Seattle area and asked herself, "Do I know anyone who works there?" As it turned out, she did know someone. In fact, it was a former client of hers. She spoke to the client and the client went right up to the human resources department. The human resources personnel immediately pulled out my friend's application, interviewed her—and guess what? She got the job! Networking works.

Nurturing Is a Two-Way Street

Now that you have a networking list it is time to nurture your network. This is about letting people know what your career goals are and also finding out what *their* interests are. It's about caring for and listening to others as they express their interests, values and goals. Get to know what your acquaintances and professional contacts like to do in their spare time. Do they have a special interest? Do they volunteer for a cause? Ask questions, listen carefully, and become well-versed in their areas of interest and expertise.

Take notes and then remember the "little" things like sending your contacts copies of newsletters, newspaper and magazine articles, reports and program materials that you think will interest them. Include a short, handwritten note that can be as simple as "FYI." If the article relates to your mutual career interests, this will raise your professional credibility because it shows that you keep abreast of industry happenings. During the holidays, send appropriate notes/cards and possibly extend an invitation to lunch for no particular reason. Send a congratulatory note to someone who has recently received a promotion or an advanced degree.

Here are some common courtesy rules to follow:

- Always respect your contacts' names. Get an "OK" before you use a person's name as a referral to meet someone else.

- Keep an eye on the clock. Respect other people's busy schedules and make sure you call at times that are convenient and appropriate for your contacts.
- Thank everyone who helps you or provides you with ideas or leads. It's wise to thank people for leads even if their suggestions do not lead directly to a desired work situation. Your contacts will appreciate the follow-up. Send them thank you cards and let them know where you are in your job search.

Joining and Participating in Professional Organizations

There are hundreds of professional organizations in most cities and larger towns. Many of them have local chapters that have open introductory meetings. You can attend once or twice to find out more about them. They might have a lunch, a dinner, or a networking breakfast. You'll find international, national, state and local organizations geared to virtually every type of industry, career field or special interest. Some are targeted or based upon:

- Broad professional disciplines (e.g., American Marketing Association)
- Industry-specific (e.g., American Film Marketing Association)
- Gender (e.g., Financial Women International)
- Ethnicity (e.g., National Black MBA Association)
- Sexual orientation (e.g., Gay and Lesbian Journalists Association)

Membership services include meetings and networking opportunities, trade shows, seminars, internships, publications, professional development, and employment referrals. Volunteering in these professional organizations gives you a role or function at an event which in turn makes networking easier. Some activities might involve volunteering to help with specific short-term projects or offering to help with meeting logistics or registration for fundraising activities, for example.

Alumni Associations

Alumni associations are another big resource for networking. If you are an alumnus, join your alumni association. Just calling someone who is an alumnus of the same college immediately gives both of you something in common. They can help you with contacts. I know someone who, just by going through her alumni association and making contacts, received three job offers.

Don't hesitate to contact organizations that you think would be unlikely to have openings. Some educational institutions are required to put out a job announcement even if they already have someone in mind for the job. If you get an interview, even if the company hires someone else, there may be an opening for you there later. If they interviewed you, they obviously thought your qualifications were good. So now they become part of your network. They may lead you to other organizations that have job openings.

Myths about Networking and Job Search Issues

Myth # 1: I went to a small school so there probably won't be many resources for job networking.

Yes, this alumni network may be smaller but at the same time it probably is a tighter network. So if you attended a two-year college or a smaller school, you might be surprised. You may find a more personal connection through a smaller school networking outreach.

Myth # 2: Someone will find a job for me, an employment agency, a college placement office, for example.

As mentioned earlier, most jobs are not well-advertised. They are hidden. So it is highly improbable that someone will find a job for you. You have to find the job—and preferably one in your chosen career that you are passionate about. But you can ask many people for help.

Myth # 3: If I have a degree, I can get a job. If I can't find a job, that means I have to go back to school.

Of course your degree is important but it doesn't guarantee you a job.

Having more education or a better degree is not necessarily going to get you the job you want. There are a lot of variables here.

Basically your success in landing a job lies in your ability to assess the totality of your life experiences and relate them to your career goals and the job opening you are pursuing. Then you need to be able to "sell" yourself to the prospective employer in the interview. Instead of thinking you have to get another degree, look at the skills you have and the ones that are transferable into different occupations. Then put your package together and market yourself.

Let me again emphasize that about 80 percent of the job openings come from the hidden job market. You might believe that finding a job is a matter of luck and it's true that very often it involves being at the right place at the right time. But you have to put yourself in the right place. You cannot wait for the phone or the doorbell to ring. You have to go out and seek your opportunity. So the people who have had luck—guess what, they made their luck happen! They made the calls, they made the contacts, they made the effort. You cannot wait for it to happen. You have to make your own luck. *Myth #4: Big companies with lots of employees are naturally going to offer you the best chances of employment.*

Absolutely not true. Look at statistics from the government. They reveal that most of the new jobs are in businesses that have fewer than a hundred employees. So don't just focus on big employers; look at the smaller companies too.

Myth #5: The cover letter is not as important as the actual résumé.

Some companies will want you to send them a cover letter with a résumé. Other companies may not ask for it. Write one anyway and please, have someone read it for content, grammar and spelling errors.

Myth #6: As long as I write a cover letter and send my résumés, I'll get an interview.

Absolutely not true. You need to follow up with a phone call after a couple of weeks. Perhaps say something like this:

"Hello, my name is Susan Smith and I've applied for a job as a technical assistant at your company. Can you tell me where you are in the interview process?" That's the key question.

Some employers are a bit slow in processing résumés, but if you call and it happens that your application or résumé is in the "I'm not so sure pile," they may take it out of the "maybe" pile and look at it again because you expressed an interest and made a connection. It puts your name in their consciousness and may cause them to take a second look.

Myth #7: Only the people that have the most qualifications get the job.

Again, absolutely not true. Yes, you have to meet certain defined minimum qualifications but if an employer likes you, he or she will hire you and train you into the position. The key is how much the employer likes you and feels that you are the right person for the job.

Myth #8: The younger person will get the job.

There are employers out there who really prefer more mature workers who have more experience, are more reliable, and won't have child-care issues.

You might hesitate to go on some interviews because you believe that the employer already has someone in mind for the job. Don't let that stop you from pursuing a job that interests you. It's true that there are educational institutions and government agencies that are required to put out a job announcement even when they have already chosen someone. Again, if you do the interview, even if the company hires someone else, there may be an opening for you later. That employer has now become part of your network and he or she may know of other job opportunities.

Strategies for Developing a Referral Campaign

The time to start putting your networking strategy to work is now. Remember these important steps:

A. Develop a general list of people, professional groups and existing networks you might access. Brainstorm with others. The list might include:

- Friends
- Relatives
- Influential leaders
- Colleagues/peers
- Faculty
- Present, past and potential employers
- People in informational services (librarians, counselors, newspaper editors, etc.)

B. Divide the list into groups of people who could give helpful suggestions, identify leads to potential positions, serve as references.

C. Determine the easiest place to start. Many people begin with friends, relatives, parents of friends, etc.

D. Develop a plan that includes gathering information through:

- leads in business articles, newspapers, journals, annual reports
- general contacts and casual conversations
- attendance at organized networks, e.g., professional organizations, civic groups, religious groups
- informational interviewing in your targeted area

E. Know the basics of informational interviewing.

1. Establish initial appointments through an introductory letter, phone call, or referral from another person.
2. Lead-ins or purpose for the contact can be varied. You may be:
    - Doing career research
    - Doing a class project
    - Seeking advice on résumé writing
    - Wanting to discuss your vocational interest
    - Wanting to present a product
    - Desiring information on a specific field, industry or geographical area.
3. Be specific about the length of time being requested. Usually 20 minutes.
4. Prepare for the interview. Read company and agency literature. Know what information you plan to request. Write out your questions which may include:
    - Duties of the person; major responsibilities
    - Functions or structure of the organization
    - Trends in the field
    - Procedures, products, programs used or being developed
    - Sources for additional information
    - Suggestions for entry and/or development into a particular position, field or company
5. Make a positive impression
    - Arrive early for your interview
    - Dress well
    - Introduce yourself to the receptionist
    - Consider having a business card

- Have a résumé and references available in case you are asked

6. Ask for referrals, others you could contact
7. Follow up with a handwritten thank you note.
8. Maintain contact by providing feedback to those with whom you have interviewed.
9. Remember, you are not asking for a job. You may indicate that you are looking for a job and would like to be considered. Your present purpose, however, is to gain information and advice from experienced and knowledgeable people.

F. Keep your contacts informed of your progress.

G. Follow up on all job leads that seem of interest by:

- using traditional methods, such as a letter or résumé.
- conducting an informational interview.
- positioning yourself in situations where you meet the individuals with position openings and make a favorable impression.

H. When attending professional groups, civic groups or established networks:

- Introduce yourself to as many individuals as possible.
- Join appropriate groups by paying membership fees.
- Serve on committees to gain exposure and to display your abilities.
- Tell others of your interests and plans.
- Distribute your business cards.
- Collect business cards from others.
- Arrange lunches to develop relationships with new contacts you meet who might be in the position to help you.

You have to put yourself out there. It's all about making contacts. Looking for a job is a full-time job. If you already have a job and are looking for a better job, of course you cannot look for a job eight hours a day. But if you are not employed, then you have four to five hours a day to job search. Consider it your job to look for work.

CHAPTER 8: CLARIFY YOUR CAREER CHOICES

This chapter has been designed specifically to address the needs of college students who may not have a lot of work experience to draw upon; however anyone embarking on a new career phase will find the self-assessment exercises provided here useful.

Choosing a career is not a simple matter today. In the past, children dreamed of growing up to be astronauts, doctors, lawyers, or teachers. Very few of them thought of being water quality technicians or tax accountants. Now new jobs and new job titles are created every day. The possibilities seem endless, even overwhelming. It was once normal for college students to declare a major related to a career, complete a prescribed set of studies, find a job in a related field, and stay in that field until they retired. One decision and that was it! Today, it is far more common for individuals to change their majors and do several career searches and changes throughout their working life. People change their careers for a variety of reasons. They may not have made a wise choice initially. Or, the career they selected no longer exists. Or, they want to match their changing values and needs to a new set of career possibilities. These are just a few examples.

Although there is no simple solution to finding the right career path for you, there are simple steps you can take utilizing all of your resources to make a good decision. Take advantage of any opportunity to consult with the important people in your life. Often other people can identify skills and qualities that you possess even if you can't see them in yourself. Discuss your questions and concerns with friends and family and, if you are a student, be sure to schedule a one-to-one appointment with the career advisor on your campus.

Now is the time to begin a self-assessment process that will give you more choices, broaden your options, and give you the confidence to know you are on the right career path. A self-assessment will clarify your characteristics, interests, values and skills. It will define your strengths and your weaknesses. Looking for a match between these and the work you are considering is the most important step you can take before you write a résumé or begin the search for a job. In fact, when the time comes to write your résumé and prepare for a job interview, you will find the task easier if you have completed the self-assessment process first!

YOU are the place to start, so ask yourself:

- What do I do well?
- What am I good at?
- What do others tell me?
- What do I enjoy doing?
- What turns me on?
- What energizes me?

Answers to these types of questions and many others will help you identify your strengths and make decisions around the contributions you can make. Many people try to fit into jobs advertised in newspapers or other sources. The employer today has many qualified candidates from which to choose. You will be seriously considered for a position only by showing the employer that you know who you are, what you can offer, and where you are going.

You will need to commit some time to prepare your personal inventory. Your honesty and the quality of your work will predict your level of success in getting the right job. Write out your answers and the conclusions you come to as a permanent record of your thoughts and feelings. This data then becomes an important resource as you continue in your career planning and work search activities.

In order to prepare for this process, the first step is to complete the Pride Experience. This exercise will enable you to lay the foundation for assessing your interests, values and skills.

Developing Your Pride List

List experiences from your past that were positive for you. These are things that you are proud of, that make you feel energized as you recall them. Include your earliest memories. They can be anything from building a house to drawing a picture or running a race. It only matters how you feel about it. The standard to use in choosing items for this list is your own pride in feeling "I did that myself." Put items down in the order that they occur to you without prioritizing them. It is ideal if you can come up with 20 to25 items. Remember, it is important to write about things you did in a variety of life roles (such as parenting, cooking, volunteering, learning as a student, etc.).

One aspect of career development is the art of prioritizing. Choose from your pride list the top seven activities according to your pride in them, joy in doing them, and level of energy in recalling them. Identify these in order of preference. Describe exactly what you did in each situation, what you accomplished, and what you enjoyed. Try to be precise if certain specific goals were reached.

Personality Checklist

After prioritizing the list and stories of what you are proud of, the next step is to identify key elements of your personality. As you review the seven stories about your successes, go to the Personality Checklist provided here and check which attributes you exhibited in your success stories. Be honest when you judge your thoughts, feelings and attitudes.

Personality Checklist

Calm	Likeable	Leader
Easy going	Honest	Likes outdoors
Risk taker	Reliable	Likes people
Accurate	Empathetic	Original
Challenging	Discreet	Perfectionist
Adventurous	Tenacious	Productive
Creative	Self-confident	Practical
Open	Perceptive	Rational
Warm	Assertive	Responsible
Objective	Sensitive	Self-starter
Outgoing	Astute	Sociable
Tactful	Diplomatic	Stable
Loyal	Receptive	Tolerant
Successful	Punctual	Trustworthy
Versatile	Competent	Talented
Adaptable	Flexible	Dependable
Democratic	Artistic	Energetic
Resourceful	Committed	Positive attitude
Determining	Compassionate	Hard worker
Patient	Dedicated	Imaginative
Innovative	Dependable	Independent
Persistent	Intelligent	Inquisitive
Enthusiastic	Intuitive	
Expressive	Kind	

Values Checklist

Next, you will want to examine your values closely. If you hope to experience career satisfaction, you will take time to examine your values and make choices that are consistent with them. This section will help you to identify what is needed in your work environment to enable you to feel satisfied with your job. Understanding your values is also essential to preventing conflict in the workplace.

Again, review your pride stories and then scan the Values Checklist provided in Chapter 4. Put a checkmark to show each value that applies to you. You can also add any values that may not be listed.

Skills Assessment

Next, you will define and identify your skills. A skill is a learned ability to do something well. Skills are the currency used by workers. In the labor market you receive pay in exchange for the skills you offer and use at work. Individuals who can describe themselves to a potential employer in terms of their skills are more likely to find the work that they want and enjoy.

If you were asked right now to list your skills, what would your list look like? It might be a short list, not because you do not have the skills, but simply because you have never been asked to identify them and are not accustomed to thinking and talking about them. Each person has approximately 700 different skills in their repertoire. Most individuals have trouble identifying them and if they do recognize them, they don't feel right promoting them. You cannot afford this kind of misdirected modesty! Before you can be confident about your ability to move through a changing work world, you have to realistically know what your strengths are.

Again, review your pride stories and then check to show each skill that you used in your personal pride stories. Circle words with which you strongly associate.

Understanding Your Career Interests

Now it's time to take a closer look at the Holland Code, which was introduced in Chapter 1. Dr. John Holland developed the Holland Code based on the theory that people and work environments could be classified into six different groups, as represented in the diagram below. You may identify with all six of the groups but you will probably identify most strongly with two or three of the groups. Determine your three-letter code based on the first letter of each group (in the order you chose them). Your code might be R-I-A, A-S-C, I-E-C, or any other possibility.

Your three-letter Holland Code can be used to explore different majors and careers. You are encouraged to focus on all three of your Holland Code letters and all of their various combinations. In addition to helping you find the career path that is right for you, your Holland Code can be useful as you make choices about participating in community service, the type of environment you would like to work in, or even the hobbies and activities you might want to pursue. As you can see, your Holland Code can be a powerful tool to jumpstart your exploration on the path to making decisions about majors and careers.

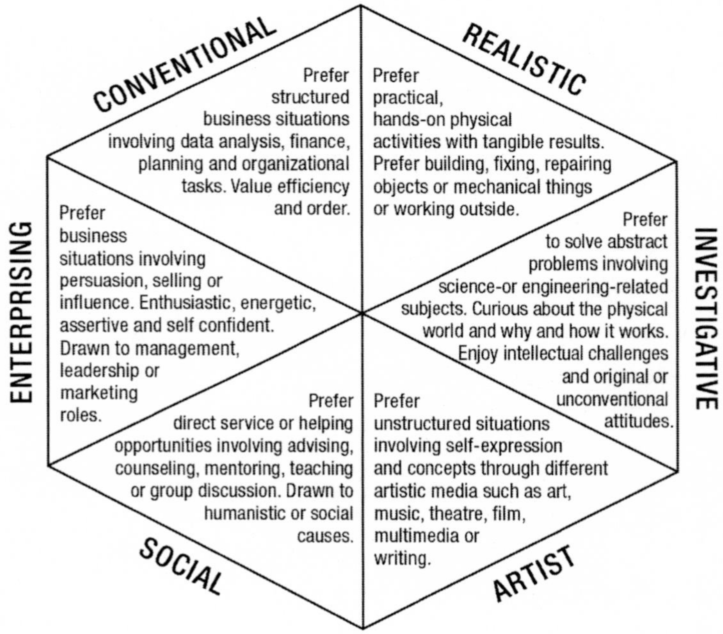

If you are a student, you have probably not had an extensive work history to help you learn about areas of interest. Therefore it is important for you to list all the ways and means you have come to know about them. For example, what courses did you enjoy in college or high school, what extracurricular activities did you take up, what kinds of books do you like to read, what trainings have you received either in the workplace, with volunteer involvement, in sports organizations, etc. Also, it is important to list what you enjoyed learning in your travels, research and other experiences.

Review your writings and list five areas of knowledge that you would like to build on in your career. Now go back to the Holland personality types and see if there are matchups with the educational preferences in each personality type with your five main knowledge areas. This process can help you to identify rewarding career pathways.

The list below matches Holland codes to career clusters. To further investigate any of the career clusters named, go to http://www.iseek.org/guide/counselors/counselorclustersholland.html

R-Realistic

- Agriculture, food and natural resources
- Architecture and construction
- Arts, A/V technology and communications
- Health science
- Hospitality and tourism
- Information technology
- Law, public safety, corrections and security
- Manufacturing
- Science, technology, engineering and mathematics
- Transportation, distribution and logistics

I-Investigative

- Health science
- Information technology
- Law, public safety, corrections and security
- Science, technology, engineering and mathematics

A-Artistic

- Arts, A/V technology and communications
- Education and training
- Hospitality and tourism
- Human services
- Marketing, sales and service

S-Social

- Arts, A/V technology and communications
- Education and training
- Government and public administration
- Health science
- Human services
- Law, public safety, corrections and security
- Marketing, sales and service

E-Enterprising

- Arts, A/V technology and communications
- Business, management and administration
- Finance
- Government and public administration
- Hospitality and tourism
- Law, public safety, corrections and security
- Marketing, sales and service

C-Conventional

- Architecture and construction
- Business, management and administration

- Finance
- Health science
- Manufacturing
- Marketing, sales and service
- Transportation, distribution and logistics

R and I - Realistic and Investigative

- Health science
- Information technology
- Science, technology, engineering and mathematics

R and A - Realistic and Artistic

- Arts, A/V technology and communications

R and S - Realistic and Social

- Health science
- Human services
- Law, public safety, corrections and security

R and E - Realistic and Enterprising

- Arts, A/V technology and communications
- Hospitality and tourism

R and C - Realistic and Conventional

- Architecture and construction
- Manufacturing
- Transportation, distribution and logistics

I and S - Investigative and Social

- Health science

A and S - Artistic and Social

- Education and training

A and E - Artistic and Enterprising

- Arts, A/V technology and communications

S and E - Social and Enterprising

- Government and public administration
- Law, public safety, corrections and security
- Marketing, sales and service

E and C - Enterprising and Conventional

- Finance
- Health science

Career Decisions Plan

Below is a list of the steps you will go through the process of deciding on a major and exploring your career options. Copy the list in your journal, providing space to note the date when you complete each step.

Exploring Majors

1. Visit the Career Development Office at your college or university for an individual Career Advising session.
2. Complete a few assessments to help identify your areas of career interest.
3. Compare the results of your assessments to the Holland Code information.
4. Review the undergraduate majors offered at your college or university and select your possibilities.
5. Meet with your faculty advisor to discuss options.

6. Consult your friends and family about what career paths they believe are a good fit for your skills and personality.
7. Consult the resources in the Career Information Library at your college or university.
8. Schedule a follow-up session with your career advisor to review your decision process.
9. Complete the Career Decision Table below, weighing the pros and cons of various choices.
10. If a Career Exploration course is offered at your college or university, consider taking it for additional assistance in your decision.
11. Make your decision.

Exploring Careers

1. Consult the "What can I do with a major in_____?" resources online or at the Career Library at your college or university.
2. Review potential job descriptions and required level of education for careers at http://online.onetcenter.org/ or www.bls.gov/oco/.
3. Look for potential job descriptions online at job search sites to find out about what you might do on the job.
4. Seek out a part-time job, internship or volunteer opportunity in your field of interest to take it for a test drive.

In your journal, create a Decision Table like the one below to use in considering the pluses and minuses of the majors you are considering.

Major or Interest	Questions/ Concerns	Information gathered	Consider (yes/no)

Create a similar Decision Table for careers that you are considering.

Career or Interest	Questions/ Concerns	Information gathered	Consider (yes/no)

More information about using the Holland Code to explore career possibilities is available in the Heidelberg College Career Decisions Handbook, which you can download at: http://www.heidelberg.edu/sites/default/files/images/jfuller/Deciding%20Handbook.pdf.

It is also important to identify your personal learning style so that you can be more in control of your own career development and learning. To discover how you learn, think about the experiences you have had in your life in which you felt you learned a great deal. Then consider the following types of learning processes and environments:

- Unstructured or highly structured environment
- Working at your own speed or working at the pace set by a teacher or group
- Learning things step-by-step or getting the big picture first
- Working alone or working in a group

- Learning in a quiet setting or with background noise
- Forming pictures in your mind, touching the object, or speaking to yourself
- Engaging in computer-based instruction/interactive multimedia
- Conducting field work or doing case studies
- Sharing thoughtful dialogue with others or listening to a lecture
- Watching videos or films
- Participating in a role play or simulation or writing in logs, journals or workbooks
- Reading about something and then trying it out or trying something out and then reading about it later

Over the past decade an increasing number of individuals have chosen self-employment or entrepreneurship as a career option. Those who are self-employed or entrepreneurs are people who create a new product or provide a service and then proceed to put form to their dream by opening a small business. Consider the following questions:

- Do you welcome challenges?
- Are you persistent?
- Is achievement important to you?
- Can you cope with uncertainty?
- Do you usually complete any task you start?
- Are you confident about your abilities?
- Do you like to be in control?
- Do you consider yourself a realistic planner?
- Are you willing to take moderate risks?
- Do you consider yourself to be organized?

If you answered yes to most of these questions, you have some of the characteristics of people who are self-employed. Additionally, in the previous dealing with the Holland types, if you identified the Enterprising type as your first, second or third preference, you may find it helpful to review this career option further.

Composite Checklist

You have now completed each of the self-assessment sections. To create a composite picture of yourself, copy the summaries from the previous exercises into your journal, listing:

- Your Top 5 Characteristics
- Your Top 5 Values
- Your Top 5 Skills
- Your 3 Holland Themes and the potential educational or occupational options they suggest
- Your Top 5 Knowledge Areas
- Additional Characteristics / Learning Styles / Entrepreneurial Traits

Your Top Strengths and Characteristics

Review the points that you wrote in the previous table. Choose the 10 most important strengths or characteristics that you believe you have and create a list in your journal called "My Top Strengths & Characteristics." These qualities form the foundation of your career.

Congratulations! You are now ready to begin identifying specific opportunities that will allow you to use your strengths.

Part 2 of finding your career path entails successful research of career trends, changes in organizational beliefs, new work alternatives.

It is important to be aware of labor market trends to adjust your career preparation to take advantage of emerging new market trends. These trends can be divided by demographics, new technologies, economic globalization, and domestic economic conditions.

By matching your strengths and interests with the needs of your fields of interest you will be able to meet your goals. One of the most effective methods of obtaining more detailed information about a particular career is to conduct an information interview with someone who holds a position that interests you. Informational interviews are beneficial because they allow you to:

- Explore careers and clarify your career goal
- Expand your professional network
- Build confidence for your job interviews
- Access the most up-to-date career information
- Identify your professional strengths and weaknesses
- See the organization from the inside

Those of you who are currently enrolled in undergraduate or graduate programs may find yourselves doing these self-assessment exercises several times as you gather more experience and information about the fields you are considering at the same time you are completing your academic work. The resources at your school offer many opportunities to help you learn, develop and grow both academically and professionally. Take advantage of all that your school has to offer as you lay the foundation for your future success.

Career Development Resources

Source: Heidelberg College Career Decisions Handbook

"Choosing a Major" Books

Career Compass, Peggy Simonsen

Career Planning Today, C. Randall Powell

Following Your Career Star, Jon Snodgrass

How to Choose a College Major, Linda Landis Andrews

Reality 101, Fran Katzanek

The Three Boxes of Life, Richard Nelson Bolles

What Color Is your Parachute? Richard Nelson Bolles

What's Your Type of Career? Donna Dunning

Your Career: Choices, Chances, Changes, David C. Birchard, John J. Kelly, Nancy Pat K. Weaver

Your Career, How to Make it Happen Julie Griffin Levitt

Major/Career Books

Careers for Good Samaritans and other Humanitarian Types, Marjorie Eberts and

Margaret Gisler

Developing a Lifelong Career in the Sports Marketplace, Greg J. Cylkowski, M.A.

50 Coolest Jobs in Sports, David Fischer

Great Jobs for Accounting Majors, Jan Goldberg

Great Jobs for Biology Majors, Blythe Camenson

Great Jobs for Business Majors, Stephen Lambert

Great Jobs for Chemistry Majors, Mark Rowh

Great Jobs for Communications Majors, Blythe Camenson

Great Jobs for Computer Science Majors, Jan Goldberg

Great Jobs for English Majors, Julie DeGalan and Stephen Lambert

Great Jobs for Environmental Studies Majors, Julie DeGalan and Bryon Middlekauff

Great Jobs for Foreign Language Majors, Julie DeGalan and Stephen Lambert

Great Jobs for History Majors, Julie DeGalan and Stephen Lambert

Great Jobs for Liberal Arts Majors, Blythe Camenson

Great Jobs for Math Majors, Stephen Lambert and Ruth J. DeCotis

Great Jobs for Physical Education Majors, Nancy Giebel

Great Jobs for Political Science Majors, Mark Rowh

Great Jobs for Psychology Majors, Julie DeGalan and Stephen Lambert

Great Jobs for Theater Majors, Jan Goldberg

Liberal Arts Jobs, Burt Nadler

Opportunities for Engineering and Computer Science Majors, Peterson's

Opportunities for Health and Science Majors, Peterson's

Real People Working In Science, Jan Goldberg

The Mulligan Guide to Sports Journalism Careers, Joseph F. Mulligan and Kevin T.

Mulligan

To Boldly Go: A Practical Career Guide for Scientists, Peter S. Fiske

Working in TV News: The Insiders Guide, Carl Filoreto and Lynn Setzer

Web Resources

Note: These urls were current at the time of publication of this book; however, please be aware that urls change frequently so that some extra searching may be required to find the resource your are looking for.

"Choosing a Major" Articles

Some Common Misperceptions about Choosing a Major http://www.psu.edu/dus/md/mdmisper.htm

Information about Different Majors

What Can I Do With a Major in ....

http://www.myplan.com/majors/what-to-do-with-a-major.php

Major Resource Kits

http://www.udel.edu/CSC/mrk.html

Major Match Sheets

http://www.career.fsu.edu/Resources/Match-Major-Sheets

Helpful Online Assessments

Major Assessment Online

http://www.mymajors.com/

Transferable Skills Survey http://duluth.umn.edu/careers/inventories/skills_test_intro.html

Skills_Search

http://www.onetonline.org/skills/

Skills Profiler

http://www.careerinfonet.org/skills/default.aspx

Skills Assessment

http://www.iseek.org/sv/12400.jsp?pg=12400

Quick Work Preference Inventory

http://www.careerperfect.com/services/free/work-preference/

Keirsey Temperament Sorter (MBTI)

http://www.keirsey.com/sorter/register.aspx

Working Out Your MBTI Type

http://www.teamtechnology.co.uk/ttlh-articl/mb-simpl.htm

MBTI Information

http://typelogic.com/

Information about Different Occupations

Career Overview - http://www.careeroverview.com/

Career Voyages - www.careervoyages.gov.com

Occupational Information Network (O*Net Online) - http://online.onetcenter.org/

Occupational Outlook Handbook - http://www.bls.gov/oco/

Career Interviews - http://www.careerfyi.com/leadership.asp

Career Counseling Websites

Occupational Outlook Handbook	Find hundreds of different types of jobs—such as teacher, lawyer, and nurse that provides information on training and education needed, earnings, expected job prospects, what workers do on the job, working conditions and links to related occupations.
MonsterTrak	Online, Monster Trak offers assistance in the job search from resume development to preparing for job interviews.
O*Net Center	A database used to explore occupations, identify current job skills (and get a list of occupations that match skills), and get a snapshot of the skills and knowledge required for selected occupation. This replaces the old Dictionary of Occupational Titles.
JobHuntersBible.com	Richard Bolles' new internet site designed to supplement the latest version of What Color is Your Parachute, the grandfather of all career planning books.
JobStar Central	Produced by the public libraries of California, it has the best overall Resume resource guide on the WWW. The Career Guides feature links to trends, news, information by career area, career planning and assessment tools from one location. The Guides for Specific Careers is very helpful as they include the best information from various university career centers, links to the Occupational Outlook Handbook, "California Career Guides", and the About Work Career Database. Salary Information and the Hidden Job Market are also included.
Career Development eManual	The online version of the second edition of this manual developed by the University of Waterloo. A useful took for university students but also for others in any stage of career planning. Topics include self-assessment in personality, aptitude and values and how to match these characteristics with potential occupations. Job hunting strategies are also explored.
Career Ideas	A guide for career titles related to 22 popular college majors from the University of Texas.
Careers.Org	Includes thousands of links to jobs, employers, businesses, education and career professionals on the web plus other career resources such as software lists, publications, resource evaluations with everything cross-referenced geographically.

Career Options by Academic Major	Kansas State University posts its own publication relating careers to college majors, and links to other similar sites on the Internet.
The Riley Guide	The Riley Guide introduces the online job search, listing many online sites and services that are useful for the job search.
Career Magazine	A career search service. It includes job postings which tend to have a technical focus and a free resume bank, there are valuable sections featuring articles devoted to college students (On Campus) and to women and minorities (Focus on Diversity).
Career One Stop	A website to locate occupation information, industry and state information. Multiple topics related to exploring the labor market, career tools, and more.
Mapping Your Future	You can explore careers, prepare for college (help with selecting a school and applying for admission), pay for college (financial aid!), and manage your money (student loans and more).
Princeton Review's Career Exploration Page	Explore careers, majors, personal style and so much more.
CollegeBoard-MyRoad	Through College Board, it helps students explore majors, find colleges, and research careers.
My Cool Center	Allows students to explore various careers while still in school. Links to various topics like hot careers, which careers are a good fit and so much more!
CareerLink	The CAREERLINK website utilizes current computer technology, the internet, interactive feedback, and instant data analysis to provide you with information supporting your career development process.
My Majors.com	MyMajors.com provides useful advice on college majors that a high school student or college freshman with your interests and achievements might enjoy and excel in. It's free!
CSU Long beach - Career Center	This link through CSU Long Beach's career center provides information on career counseling, choosing a major, career planning, graduate school, career workshops and resources.
UCLA Career Guide	A Guide through UCLA's Career Center on career planning, job strategies, resumes, interviewing and more.
Careers & Colleges	This website offers advise on Majors and Careers. We help with advice and tools you can really use - from self-assessment tests to help with finding your first job.

Source: College of the Canyons - http://www.canyons.edu/

The Importance of Self-Assessment

Whether you are a college student with little or no work history or an experienced worker seeking a new career direction, finding your way through the maze of career options available today can be daunting unless you have clarity about the choices that are appropriate for you. This clarity can be gained only through careful and honest self-assessment of your personality, your values your strengths and your skills.

CHAPTER 9: RETIRE WITH FIRE!

When the concept of "retirement" with a pension was formulated in the 1880s in Germany (and in the 1920s in the United States), only a small percentage of the population lived long enough to collect the pension. Now, for the first time in history, most people can expect to be in "retirement" for 15 to 30 years. It is generally accepted that after the stages of growing up (from birth to age 20) and building a career and family (from age 20 to age 60), retirement is now considered a wonderful new stage called "the Bonus Years." We have this gift of time, combined with our skills and talents, to create the best stage of life for ourselves. The greatest mistake, however, is thinking that our retirement years will be happy and perfect without any planning or preparation. It's magical thinking that will lead to depression, disappointment, and even declining health. This chapter is about how, when you're approaching your retirement years, you can reinvent yourself and allow or effect a transformation into a fulfilling new life.

People today have more money at retirement than their parents had and they are living longer and healthier lives. As new retirees we have or will have so many choices available to us that were undreamed of by past generations of senior citizens. For the current and future generations of people leaving the full-time workforce, retirement will not carry the same meaning as in previous generations. This is due in part because of the unique factors mentioned above but also because our generation is much more knowledgeable and sophisticated and has more of an awareness and need to contribute.

We no longer want to "retreat" or "withdraw" into endless days of leisurely activities that yield little meaning or purpose. Many people in their 50's and 60's are looking for a kind of "renaissance," to discover what gives their lives true meaning outside of their work life. Many consider travel abroad for pleasure, educational opportunities, or to better the world by volunteering at the different international agencies that are available. Others will volunteer locally to make a difference in social services with which they feel a kinship, both as a way to contribute and also as a way to stay connected to a larger community—a goal that is vital to anyone who wants to remain healthy throughout their retirement years.

Many men and women plan to keep working—for a variety of reasons—well into their late 60s and 70s. Some retirees will gradually leave the full-time workforce and decrease their hours for an employer. Some will choose to become consultants, working whenever and as much as they wish. Others will seek out educational opportunities to expand their knowledge or take up a new hobby, This chapter will help you retire successfully so that you can have a satisfying life after you leave the nine-to-five work-a-day world. To have a quality retirement, you need to incorporate the qualities and elements you would miss most from your work life as you enter into your retirement. You need to explore your interests and be ready to discover and experiment with new ways of thinking, behaving and engaging with others, based on your self-exploration. The questions and exercises in this chapter will help to stimulate a dialogue within yourself as well as between you and significant others so that you can extract new understanding about your needs and wants and gain a sense of what you would like to pursue in the future. The goal is for you to have the best possible retirement.

For some people, they have actually *become* their jobs; their work has evolved to the point of defining who they are as a person. This restricted sense of *who* we are will hinder our sense of self-esteem as we move into the retirement years where work is less important or is no longer available to us. The question of "Who am I?" can no longer be largely defined by what we do. It becomes an exploration centered on our intrinsic values. This internalized search is usually not easy or familiar to most of us. It requires taking time to reflect honestly in order to create a more comfortable and realistic self-definition. Retirees who cannot redefine themselves will default to a more dependent, passive way of living and will stop growing emotionally and psychologically. Ask yourself, "How much time have I spent addressing this issue of redefinition?"

Understanding the Benefits of Work

This exercise will help you recognize the benefits from work beyond receiving a paycheck. It is generally accepted that work brings most people five basic benefits:

1. Financial stability
2. Ability to have a structured week (time management)
3. A sense of purpose
4. Opportunity to be social with others
5. Status.

Part 1: Consider how well your current work situation meets the above needs on a scale of 1 to10. Add a brief description of how your present work environment serves to fulfill the five basic benefits listed here.

Part 2: Review how in your retirement you will successfully be able to replace these five functions of work. Rating from 1 to 10, how successfully you feel these work functions can be replaced.

In taking your first steps to retirement, ask yourself, "To what degree do I feel I am emotionally detached from the strivings and accomplishments of the work I am about to leave behind?" How much do you see yourself defined by your work? How much is your personal worth invested in your work world?

By reflecting on these questions you will gain a clearer understanding of what you need to do to redefine and redesign your life in the process of retiring. Even if you plan to continue working on a part -time basis, your leisure time will increase. So you will be focusing on making a smooth transition from full-time work to more leisure time. After you have explored the qualities you highly enjoyed in the workplace, consider ways to fulfill those same needs in your increased leisure time. This will make your transition much less stressful and uncertain.

The Five Stages of Retirement

It has been observed that there are basically five stages to retirement. By understanding these stages you will find it easier to deal with the emotional component of retirement, a pivotal transition from an active work life to creating an identity outside the work environment. These are:

Stage 1. Anticipation–Before retiring you may experience emotions ranging from euphoria to anxiety as you think about what you will finally be able to do as well as the amount of uncertainty that each day may bring if it is not so highly structured by work. This is the planning stage, a time for considering how you will bring your dreams into fruition as you gradually disengage emotionally and physically from your work-a-day life. This stage begins well before you retire. In one recent poll (Thestreet.com from Yahoo finance), it was found that only 44 percent of those polled felt that they were on track for a fulfilling retirement.

Stage 2. Enchantment–Upon retiring you may feel like you are on a vacation and are greatly relieved of the burden of work-related responsibilities. This stage may last a few months to several years. If you have not designed your retirement well, however, this stage may be followed by boredom, anxiety or disenchantment as you meander without purpose through most of your retirement.

Stage 3. Disappointment–After vacationing for a while, a feeling of depression may surface if you are not addressing your need for a focused, meaningful life. Many retirees do have a list of projects they want to complete but usually retirement will greatly outlast most "to do" lists. Approximately 30 to 40 percent of retirees are depressed within the first years of retirement. This can lead to health problems if unattended.

Stage 4. Refocusing–Now it is time to intentionally plan for the rest of your life. What brings meaning to you? What makes you happy? What essentials do you miss from your work life and how can you have more of those qualities in your retirement? What do you wish you could do now? Some people take community college courses, volunteer, start up a consulting practice, take up hobbies, rekindle family relationships and friendships. Embrace the spirit of risk-taking when going into new learning experiences. Create a new vision for yourself and develop an action plan to make your retirement dreams come true. Ask yourself, "If I knew I couldn't fail what would I do next?"

It's important to look at what has satisfied you in work situations. Is it a sense of accomplishment? Is it the feeling of belonging or receiving recognition? Once you have determined what has given you an emotional payoff in your work life then you can transfer that understanding to activities that will satisfy you in retirement. Consider also what kind of social network you enjoy for your activities as well as the manner in which you like to receive recognition or positive feedback. These three components—satisfying activities, a strong social network, and the opportunity for recognition—can contribute to a high degree of fulfillment in retirement. This stage of refocusing can appear between two to 15 years into retirement.

Stage 5. A Rewarding Retirement–This stage, with intentional forethought and design, will yield a healthy and balanced life. The retiree who achieves this is open to new sources of learning and exploration and carries a deepening sense of life's purpose while nurturing rich, rewarding relationships. It's never too late to be who you might have been. It's never too late for a second childhood where you can explore without interruption yearnings and passions in the arts, in service work, in new areas of interest. Retirement can then be experienced as an adventure, a process of experimentation in bringing out the best in ourselves and our interaction with others. One poll (Agewave.com) showed 75 percent of those interviewed claiming to enjoy retirement with less worry and depression 16 years into this stage.

It is hoped that through honest self-reflection in designing (or redesigning) your retirement, you can more easily move through Stages 1, 2 and 3 to use the Refocusing Stage to achieve a more rewarding retirement. There can be a number of reasons why people become disenchanted with retirement. First, they may have retired for the wrong reasons. Then without a plan they become overwhelmed by boredom, finding that the rest and leisure activities were not enough. Secondly, if they had no realization of the emotional component of retiring, coupled with a general lack of self-scrutiny and no real retirement plan, they become distressed, especially if they had no more meaningful reason to connect to their community. Third, some assume that the retirement process will unfold naturally and that they won't have to do the work of intentionally designing their retirement. Let's avoid these pitfalls by dong an exercise that will take you on a journey that enables you to retire with fire.

Determine how ready you are to retire by copying the following questions in your journal and noting, on a scale of 1 to 10 (1 being "not ready" and 10 being "It's in place—done"), the appropriate number for your state of readiness to retire with ease.

1. What is your attitude about aging?

1 = Aging means depression, declining health and assets

10 = Aging means "I am optimistic, feel great, take good care of myself, travel, do not judge or allow others to judge me by my age, learn new activities without the interruptions of raising a family or going to work."

2. What are your financial resources?

1 = I do not have any money to retire on now. I must keep working.

10 = I have planned for retirement, and the money is there for me when I need it.

3. What are your engagement plans?

1 = I don't know what I'm going to do with my time. I'm a loner.

10 = I am looking forward to being a volunteer, entrepreneur, assistant, student, learner.

4. How strong is your marriage or social network?

1 = I do not have a healthy marriage. I do not have many friends.

10 = I have a loving intimate partner. I have a strong circle of supportive friends.

5. Do you like your retirement location?

1 = I don't like my place of residence now. It's too cold, too hot, too expensive, too remote.

10 = I love my place of retirement. It meets all my environmental needs.

6. Do you have leisure activities?

1 = I don't know what to do with my time. I don't do anything well.

10 = I can choose from many activities that I highly enjoy doing.

7. Do you have good health?

1= I have poor health that limits my resources and options for satisfying retirement.

10 = I keep myself healthy through a balance of good diet, exercise, sleep and emotional well-being.

8. Do you have an identity/purpose (outside of the work world)?

1 = I've always identified with being a worker or "workaholic."

10 = I have interests, meaning and values outside of my work life.

The more 10s you recorded, the higher your chances of having a successful retirement. Review those issues where you scored the lowest and begin creating an action plan for designing a healthy response for that category in order to have a happier time in your retirement.

(Source: Richard Johnson, Retirement Options)

Strengths are used to accomplish something in the outer world, but employing your strengths also gives you inner strength. When you use your strengths you stay engaged in healthy ways which is the key to a happier retirement. In order to have a fulfilling retirement you do need to reflect on your personal strengths. Strengths, when employed, are effortlessly tapped into; they are the skills or qualities that flow from you naturally or effortlessly. Some examples of strengths are creativity, leadership, honesty, fairness, persistence, or perspective.

Write down five strengths that are core to your nature, strengths that you use almost unconsciously. Record how you have used each strength, this fundamental skill, in your work environment. For example, if you wrote that persistence was a strength, you might say that completing all parts of a project on time was an example of your persistence. Now write how you will use that strength in your retirement. For example, you could learn a new language until fluent enough to travel abroad. Or you could work toward a health goal.

Finally, ask yourself, "What is my personal view of retirement?" Will you judge yourself as being incompetent? Disengaged from the "real world?" Devalued by your family or society? Engaged in meaningless activities due to limited finances or physical capabilities? Or will you look at the other side of the spectrum and see that retirement can be a truly exciting time to learn and be involved with activities that really matter to you?

We can live from choice and design even in retirement and nurture positive attributes in ourselves as well as others. Look back at your answers and consider how realistic your beliefs are about retirement. How can you change the beliefs that are unrealistic or inaccurate? What contributions are you ready to make in creating a successful retirement?

Ten Ways to Retire the Word "Retirement"

(Source: Howard Stone, 2Young2Retire)

1. Retire the word "retirement" from your vocabulary. Look it up: It means to "withdraw" or "retreat." Words can shape reality and it's time for this one to go. Doesn't "renaissance" or "graduation" better describe your post-career life?
2. Realize that retirement is a relatively new concept in human evolution. A few generations ago, before social security and full-time leisure became culturally embedded as the "norm," elders remained productive members of society relied upon for their insight, wisdom and skills.
3. Restructure your priorities around what is most important to you like deepening relationships with family and friends, community service, or the arts. Now is the time to bring your professional life into line with your deeper values.
4. Renew your zest for education. The learning cells of your brain are hungry for new and stimulating challenges and the welcome mat is out at many schools and universities.
5. Revitalize your energy by finding a community of people who embrace growth and change. Don't get stuck with the "been there, done that" crowd.
6. Rekindle your spirit for risk-taking. "Do not fear mistakes," said jazz immortal Miles Davis, "there are none." If not you, then who? If not now, when?
7. Respond to new opportunities. Remain open to the infinite possibilities the world has to offer. Your full potential may lie ahead.
8. Recharge your system by moving your body regularly. Walk, dance, swim, do yoga, take up hiking or biking. Find something you really enjoy and make it a part of your daily wellness program.
9. Revisit your childhood dreams. It's never too late to be who you might have been. Go for it!

10. Remember that the wisdom to discover and act on your deepest passion is within you.

Looking at the areas where you've had success in your life so far will help you think about the kind of future life you want to create.

Your Unique Success Identity

(Source: Retirement Options © 2001 Richard P. Johnson, Ph.D.)

You have a special way that you create the successes in your life. Not all of your successes follow the same theme or pattern, but most do. What are the themes and patterns of the successes you have had in your life?

1. How did you do it?
2. What motivated you?
3. Who did you do it with?
4. When did you do it?
5. Where were most of your successes?
6. In what life arena did you have most of your successes?

Past Life Successes

In your journal, create a chart like the one below to identify the successes you have had (both public and private) in the decades of your life.

Age	Success	Public	Private
0-10			
11-20			
21-30			
31-40			
41-50			
51-60			
61-70			
70+			

Once you know where and how you were successful, be sure to incorporate and use these skills and strengths in your retirement. Believe me, you will end up being happier and more fulfilled.

In retirement we have the freedom to do what we truly love. So do what you love by being of service to others, teaching others to do what you love, writing about what you love, speaking about what you love, creating a product that you love, selling or promoting what you love, or setting up, repairing, or maintaining what you love. Retirement is an open, vast horizon ready to hold all the connections and activities that you have been wanting to be involved with but were too busy to engage in for most of your life. Now the sky is the limit! Retire with fire!

CHAPTER 10 : FIND OUT WHERE YOU FIT

The previous sections of this book have focused on helping you, the reader, to consider some basic questions: "What are my skills, talents, strengths, values, interests, and personal qualities and how will they fit into the workplace?" The answers to these questions help you define who you are in relation to your search for the career path that will bring you the most fulfillment. The next part of this journey is finding out what actually is available in the world of work. This is the time for occupational research and exploration.

Fortunately there are many ways to do research. The internet has become a professional necessity today. It provides almost limitless resources for learning what jobs are available in your area as well as what skills are needed. Not only does it offer the ability to conduct an online job search and put you in touch with thousands of career opportunities, it can also showcase to employers your adaptability to change, ability to learn new tools of the trade, and initiative in keeping your technology skills current.

Although the internet is a powerful tool to add to your job search arsenal, don't neglect traditional strategies such as networking, company research, a winning résumé, and thorough interview preparation. Take advantage of resources such as:

Professional and Trade Publications–There are thousands of magazines, journals, and newsletters with information about specific fields or industries which may also contain job listings.

Newspaper Advertisements–By analyzing ads you can unearth valuable information relating to today's job market. You may want to consider subscribing to a major newspaper in your chosen area when involved in a long-distance job search. You can learn of current salaries, pick up buzzwords to use in cover letters and at interviews, and find out which skills, qualifications, degrees and work experiences to emphasize in your résumé and cover letter. Some newspapers provide web pages where they include jobs that were advertised in recent editions.

Job Search Jump Starts—Libraries are a bountiful source of information about career development and labor markets. There are also public and private employment agencies along with career centers on and off college campuses. These career centers provide vital resources to help you become familiar with job specific required skill sets, specific "language" inherit in each field, range of salary, pathways to promotions.

Governmental Listings–Federal, state and local government agencies generally publish lists of open positions. Find out how frequently the lists are updated. If civil service exams are required, find out exam dates. Prepare for and take the required tests for jobs you are interested in. Get on the registry if one is used in the hiring process.

Employment Agencies–If you are using an employment agency, investigate the quality of their services by asking other users and checking the local Chamber of Commerce and Better Business Bureau. Contact employers you would like to work for and find out what agencies they use.

Executive Recruiters–Executive recruiters rarely work with candidates who send them unsolicited résumés. The best way to get executive recruiting firms to notice you is to involve yourself in professional and community activities and networking groups where you will be visible to recruiters and their referral sources. If you choose to pursue a more direct approach, send a résumé with a cover letter only to targeted search firms that work in your industry, explaining what you want in your next position. Suggest that the recruiter contact you whether she has a search assignment matching your qualifications or not, since you know a number of people who might meet her needs and you're happy to help. Then follow up with a phone call to see if you can be of service.

Career Fairs

If you are looking for career ideas or actively pursuing a full-time job, it is definitely worth your while to attend career fairs. The relaxed and friendly "open house" format makes it easy to ask questions, explore career options, develop a network of professional contacts, identify job openings, and sometimes even land an interview—all in one location. You can discuss basics such as work experience, internships, skills and accomplishments, educational credentials, extracurricular activities, volunteer work, awards and honors. Remember to keep track and write notes of which résumé you give to each employer.

Advertise yourself. Consider your interaction at the career fair as the first round of a job interview. Be ready with a thumbnail sketch of skills and talents that set you apart from the other applicants who are competing for the same job. Rehearsing your pitch to friends, family or even a mirror will make you feel and appear more confident, organized and focused. Looking and acting professional when interacting with a recruiter demonstrates your professionalism as an employee. Greet recruiters with confidence and enthusiasm as you offer a firm, friendly handshake and make eye contact to establish rapport. You should try to dress professionally for the fair but if you have work or school before the fair and can't change clothing, you should still attend. The opportunity to meet and interact with recruiters is most important and be sure to get business cards of all those you talk with. You can then use them to call back as a follow-up.

Informational Interviews

The informational interview has become a standard practice for job seekers today. It can be an excellent tool for exploring your options and increasing your career knowledge. Informational interviews are one of the best ways to find out if a particular career choice would be beneficial for you. An informational interview is a highly focused information gathering session with a networking contact. It is designed to help you choose or refine your career path by giving you an insider'spoint of view.

What are the benefits of conducting an Informational Interview? The concept of "informational interviewing" was conceived by Richard Nelson Bolles, author of the best- selling career development book *What Color Is Your Parachute?* Bolles describes the process as "... trying on jobs to see if they fit you." He notes that most people choose a career path without taking the time to speak with professionals in their field of interest. As a result they find themselves in careers not truly matched to their skills, values, interests and abilities. Informational Interviews are opportunities to:

- Gather valuable information from industry professionals on career planning and job search strategies.
- Discover the realities of a particular career field and what it is really like to work in a given industry.
- Evaluate whether a career is compatible with your skills, interests, lifestyle, and goals.
- Receive specific suggestions on how and where to acquire the experience and knowledge required.
- Develop confidence in interviewing with professionals by discussing your interests and goals.
- Gain access to the hidden job market. Over 80 percent of quality jobs are secured through networking.
- Expand your network of contacts in your field of interest for future opportunities.
- Gain referrals to other professionals in the same field for additional networking. You can get an informational interview via a friend or acquaintance or through a referral in a networking relationship and from alumni associations of the university you graduated/will graduate from. Many career counselors recommend a written request followed by a phone call. This professional and respectful approach can bring a more favorable response.

The letter you send serves as a preliminary introduction to help communicate your intention for information only. When you call for the interview, refer to the letter you sent and follow these basic guidelines for setting up an informational interview:

- Say who you are and why you want to get together.
- Make it clear you are not asking for a job.
- Mention a personal referral or mutual interest to stimulate conversation.
- Ask for a brief meeting (about 20 minutes) at a time that's convenient to the contact, letting the person know you are considering going into the field he or she is gainfully employed in.

To prepare for the interview:

- Read about the career area and organization with which the person you are interviewing is affiliated.
- Review any available materials for background information on the industry or career field.
- Check the company or organization's website.
- Know your own interests, skills and values and how they relate to the career field represented by the person you are interviewing.
- Prepare and rehearse an opening statement that gives a brief profile of who you are and your interest in the field.
- Develop a number of thoughtful, open-ended questions to stimulate a meaningful discussion.
- If you meet face-to-face, dress appropriately in interview attire. You want to give a good first impression and look like someone who could be an asset to the profession even though you're just gathering information that day.

- Remember that preparation is the key to success. In advance of the meeting you should prepare as you would for a traditional interview. You will want to have your questions written out.

Here is a brief list of some of the basic questions to ask:

- What do you do as a …? (Fill in the title of the position of the person you are interviewing.)
- How do you spend a typical day or week?
- Do you spend most of your time at your desk? Moving around the company or out in the field?
- What kinds of problems do you deal with?
- What kinds of decisions do you make? What are your major responsibilities? What hours do you normally work?
- Is there much travel involved?
- What is the job title of the person you report to?
- What are the titles of people who report to you?
- What do you find most satisfying about your job?
- What are the positive and/or challenging aspects of working in this field?
- If you could start all over again, would you choose the same career path? Is your career path typical? If not, what might a beginner expect today?
- What are the entry level jobs in this field or organization?
- What career paths are generally available?
- What are the major responsibilities of this position?
- What skills and education are needed to enter this field?
- What kind of an entry level job or internship do you think is a good training ground?
- What are the newest developments in this field?

- What trends and developments do you see affecting career opportunities?
- What is the corporate culture of your company? Is it formal or informal?
- Do people work autonomously or in teams?
- Can you share advice with me on how to transition into this field?
- Have you been active in any professional organizations?
- Are students encouraged to participate in these organizations?

During the conversation you will be exploring what the person you are interviewing likes and doesn't like about his or her work and learning about the everyday tasks of the job. Informational interviews put you in control. You are doing the interviewing, you are not being interviewed. You are not asking for work. Most successful people will be willing to give you a realistic overview of their average work day. Also by going to their work site you get to see what kind of environment they work in. Once you've finished with the interview you ask them, "Do you know anyone else I can talk to about this field?" This is another great way to build your network. After the interview be sure to send a formal thank-you letter to the person you interviewed. It's a nice touch to share with them the results of any project or suggestion discussed during the interview and inform them what steps you have taken to apply the advice you received.

After the interview, it's important to follow up with these steps:

Report back to anyone who gave you a lead. This is not only common courtesy, it helps keep others interested and involved in your career plans and job search.

Continue to maintain contact with the person you interviewed. Keep in touch by sending an occasional article on a business-related topic that you think would be of interest or a quick note updating them on your current activities.

Later on, if you decide to pursue the career field you may wish to send out a "feeler" letter along with your progress report by stating something like, "If you hear of any job possibilities, I am enclosing my résumé and would appreciate hearing from you. Thank you so much for your time and consideration."

Job Shadowing and Volunteering

Another good step to take toward making a career decision is to "job shadow" someone for a few hours. Follow the person around and see exactly what he or she does. This will give you a really good feeling of whether or not this occupation and work environment reflect your work values.

Volunteering or doing a short internship at an organization where you would consider working is also another viable way to uncover the benefits as well as the downsides of a particular workplace. Volunteering also offers many opportunities to learn new skills that might be useful to put in your résumé.

Volunteering is especially beneficial if you have been laid off from your former job and are still "reeling" from wondering what to do with your new career choices. Volunteering can take your mind off of the negative thoughts and bring you to a better place of giving and caring for others. Building networks while volunteering is important too. You might just meet your next employer through community service work. Just get yourself out there!

The 30-Second Networking Commercial

Networking can be easy and more comfortable for you if you have a 30-second commercial prepared. Also known as an "elevator speech," the commercial is a short synopsis of your skills and experience in a format that could be delivered in the length of time you might spend going between floors with someone you met in an elevator. It is your first chance to introduce yourself with the goal of getting the listener to ask you for more information. Commercials are made to sell things and you are marketing your strengths and talents to potential employers.

The 30-second commercial is good for introducing yourself at networking or industry events as well as when talking to recruiters or hiring managers at career fairs. Take the time to develop your script so that you are comfortable talking with anyone. Your speech should be memorable and effective and create interest on the part of the listener.

These are the main elements of the networking commercial:

Who am I? What value do I bring? What elements of my past experience come together in the job I want now? What specific achievement summarizes who I am in relation to the job I want now? Identify yourself in terms of a job function or value you can contribute. What benefits might you bring to an organization based upon your strengths and qualities and proven accomplishments?

End your commercial with a question that will stimulate further action and/or referral.

Here are some do's and don'ts for the 30-second commercial:

DO:

- Focus on your strengths and assets that you would like to use in your career.
- Mention the type of industry with which you have an interest.
- Practice the commercial so you can deliver it effortlessly while appearing natural and sincere.
- Be sure that what you're saying can be backed up with facts and results.
- Use your 30-second commercial when leaving voicemails for contacts and recruiters.
- Have more than one version. Different events and situations will require you to discuss different things,

- Ask the people you speak with if there is anyone else they would recommend that you contact regarding your interests

DON'T:

- Use industry jargon or acronyms.
- Ramble. If you run out of things to say, ask a question such as, "Is there anything else you would like to know about me?" or "Would you like me to talk more about my experience?"
- Don't forget to ask for a business card, the name of a person you can follow up with, or advice for future action you should take.

Begin creating your 30-second commercial by asking the following questions:

Questions	Sample Answers
Identity: Who are you?	"I am currently a sophomore majoring in English. I have a 3.5 GPA and serve as Editor of the campus newspaper."
Traits: What are your best attributes?	"I am highly detailed and enjoy writing."
Benefits: Why you?	"I have some relevant professional experience. I interned for *The Washington Post* for two summers as a copy editor.
Intention: What are you looking for?	"I am seeking an opportunity with a travel magazine that will utilize my editorial and writing skills and enable me to travel.

After you have engaged the person in dialogue, make sure to thank him or her for taking time to talk with you and offer information. If you would like another referral you can ask the following: "Would you happen to know of anyone who would be interested in hearing more about my qualifications?"

Practice! The more you practice this and revise your commercial to fit your style, the more effective it will become for you!

Identifying and Researching Employers

The competitive advantage in the job market goes to candidates who do their homework. You'll be ahead in identifying career fields that meet your needs, targeting potential companies and succeeding on the interview. Employer research will help you: 1) Decide if you are interested in working for a particular company or organization; 2) find out about different career paths available if you are hired; and 3) prepare for an interview.

The more you know about employers in your field of interest, the stronger and more focused your job search will be. Here is the type of information you should look for:

- The Basics: Products and services, organizational structure, operating divisions and subsidiaries, location of plants and facilities, international operations, major competitors, training and development programs, and typical career paths.
- Performance and Personnel: Size and number of employees, accomplishments, sales, financial performance, research and development activities, employee diversity, and hiring and promotion policies.
- Philosophy and Culture: Mission statement, goals and objectives, traditional values, beliefs, views and operating styles that characterize the organization and the impact of private or family ownership on possible advancement potential.
- Plans for the Future: Expansion and restructuring plans, new projects, projected financial growth and new market ventures, and downsizing activities.

With a bit of resourcefulness and elbow grease you can find considerable information about many industries, employers and career opportunities. The internet has become a valuable tool for researching companies.

Here are some tips on researching public and private companies:

- Use the internet to locate corporate websites.

- Consult directories, such as *Hoover's Handbook of American Business*, *Hoover's Handbook of Emerging Companies*, and *The Almanac of American Employers*. These and other reference books are available at local libraries, college career centers, university libraries. Today many of these reference books are also online.
- Call, write or visit the company to request an Annual Report to Stockholders, sales brochures and recruiting literature.
- Contact the local Chamber of Commerce for information, particularly if the company you're interested in is small or privately owned.
- Search periodical indexes for articles in newspapers, business publications and professional journals. *The Wall Street Journal* provides a quick and insightful overview of the business world and global economy.
- Talk to company representatives at career fairs and professional association meetings.

More Job Search Strategies

Here are some additional strategies that might be appropriate for some individuals:

- **Mass Mailings**–Some job seekers may want to consider sending out mailings using firms that provide mailing lists and type in names and addresses for customized letters. If you believe this might be a good strategy for the type of service you offer, be careful to analyze the time and cost involved. Know your audience and how best to present the product: yourself. Use high-grade paper and coordinated stationery and envelopes, and address letters to names, not titles. Keep a master list of the letters and dates you mail for follow-up purposes.
- **Targeted Mailings**–To do a more targeted mailing, use the telephone to obtain information on names and titles if you cannot obtain them

through current directories. Develop a lead statement for use when calling to introduce yourself.

- **Cold Calls**–In applying to some small businesses you may feel that the best approach is to present yourself in person. If you decide to do this, be sure to arrive at a time when your energy is best. Avoid Mondays which are usually busy for many employers. Dress well to make a positive impression. Practice your communication skills and opening lines. Be sure to bring résumés and reference information with you.
- **Developing a Position**–Perhaps you have an idea for a position that suits your interests and skill set and you are aware that such a position doesn't exist at a company that you would like to work for. This may be an opportunity for you to submit a written proposal to create that position. Be sure that the position really is an answer to the company's needs and include market research and support documentation. Identify specific reasons as to why you should be the one to design and implement the program, idea or product. Claim your program/product/idea so that it is not pirated by someone else.

Through careful research you will gain a realistic picture of the job opportunities that are out there along with a good sense of what employers are looking for. By combining that knowledge with your understanding of your own career goals, you will be ready to take the plunge into a dedicated search for fulfilling work in your chosen field.

CHAPTER 11 : JUMP INTO YOUR JOB SEARCH

If you have done your homework in assessing your own values, skills and strengths and researching the current job market, you will find that these next steps in your job search will help you build the confidence you will need as you begin approaching potential employers.

The Résumé

A résumé has become an essential part of the work search process. A résumé is:

- A systematic assessment of your skills in terms of a specific work objective.
- A marketing device used to gain an interview.

The purpose of the résumé is to get an interview. It is like an advertisement: it should attract attention, create interest, describe accomplishments, and invite a person to contact you. The average amount of time an employer takes to initially scan a résumé is 30 seconds. It is very important that it be brief, one page if possible and two pages at the most. The résumé tells a potential employer what you can do and have done in the past, who you are and what you know. It also states what kind of work you seek. The key is that the résumé must provide enough information for the employer to evaluate your qualifications and become interested in inviting you for an interview.

Some sample formats for résumés are available at

http://www.careeronestop.org/ResumesInterviews/ResumeAdvice/SamplesTemplates.aspx

The Cover Letter

You may be in contact with several hundred people during your career exploration and work search activities. If you do not already know it, obtain the name and title of the person to whom you should write and be sure that you have the correct spelling. Telephone the organization to be sure your information is current. Use Ms. to address a woman unless you know that she prefers Miss or Mrs. Your correspondence will be better received when addressed to the correct person and not to a job title.

Decide on the focus of your letter, tailor your information to the reader, and make sure that all the points keep on topic.

Base your correspondence to employers around what you can do for them, not on what you want them to do for you. One page is the maximum for letters. Let your enthusiasm be apparent. You do not want to lose the reader's interest before he or she finishes the page. Avoid the words "as you can see," because the reader may not be able to "see" the point the way you do.

Check your first draft for the number of times you have written "I." Overuse of "I," monotony of sentence structure, and rambling, boring text defeat your goal of writing an effective letter. Try to limit your paragraphs to no more than four or five sentences and your sentences to a maximum of two lines. The first sentence in a paragraph introduces the topic to be covered in that paragraph.

Send an original not copies that look mass-produced. Keep a copy of your correspondence. Follow up at the appropriate time because the person to whom you have written may not contact you.

For help in writing various kinds of cover letters, thank you letters and letters for terminating discussions and accepting or rejecting an offer go to: http://www.monstertrak.com. Résumés, prospecting letters and networking letters are also covered on this site. You must create an account in order to access this information. Another good site dealing with cover letters and other job search letters is: Virginia Tech Career Services: http://www.career.vt.edu/JobSearchGuide/CoverLetterSamples.html.

The Interview

The interview is a mutual exchange of information between an employer and a candidate for a position. The primary objectives are to:

- Supply information about yourself that is not contained in your résumé.
- Show that you understand yourself and have a sense of direction in your career.
- Enable the employer to evaluate your personality and attitudes in terms of the demands of the organization and the position.
- Allow you to gain information about the organization and the job that is not available through other sources.
- Give you and the employer an opportunity to discuss the desirability of further contact or an offer of employment.

To impress an employer, you must be well prepared and understand the value of what you have to offer. To relate your assets to the position and the organization, you must know yourself. Rather than only trying to determine at what level you are currently functioning, some interviewers want to see how you have grown over time in areas related to their position(s) (e.g., interpersonal and work skills, motivation). Some interviewers will want you to talk about your mistakes to find out what you have learned to do differently.

You must be familiar with the position and the organization so that you can demonstrate how and why you will be an effective worker. Refer to the notes you made as you networked with people and reviewed print and online materials (see Section 4: Networks & Contacts).

Obtain information, if you can, on the person you will be meeting with and the schedule for the interview period. If you can find out about your interviewer(s) (e.g., name, title, background) in advance, you will be able to use this information during the interviews.

Your success or failure in the interview can depend on your appearance and the interviewer's first impression of you. If it is not good it will be much harder during the rest of the interview to change the interviewer's mind. Look neat, clean and well- groomed. Select proper clothing for the type of organization interviewing you. If in doubt, be conservative. It is also important to pay attention to details such as making sure your hands are manicured, making sure shoes (and handbags) are in good shape and keeping accessories to a minimum. If you smoke, do not smoke once you are dressed for your interview and don't drink coffee or eat odorous foods prior to your interview. Avoid wearing strong scents (e.g., perfume or cologne).

Greet each person in the company with respect and professionalism. Upon meeting the person interviewing you, give them the first opportunity to shake hands. When you shake hands include eye contact and a smile. Handshakes should be firm but not aggressive, try to match the grip of the interviewer. Do not sit down until the interviewer invites you to do so.

Don't worry if you are nervous during the interview—this is normal and will be expected. Just remember, the interviewer wants to hire you if you have the right qualifications and interest in the position. Many interviewers will begin the interview with some "small talk" to help you relax. This may seem irrelevant to the position but you are still being evaluated. Take these opening moments to show a positive attitude.

The next phase of the interview consists of the interviewer asking you questions to try to determine your fit. Having knowledge of possible questions the employer may ask enables you to prepare points to include in your answers. Think about why the question is being asked. What does the employer really want to know? The following are typical questions an employer may ask:

- Tell me about yourself.

- What are your short-term goals? What about in two and five years from now?
- What is your own vision/mission statement?
- What do you think you will be looking for in the job following this position?
- Why do you feel you will be successful in this work?
- What other types of work are you looking for in addition to this role?
- What supervisory or leadership roles have you had? What experience have you had working on a team?
- What have been your most satisfying/disappointing experiences?
- What are your strengths/weaknesses?
- What kinds of problems do you handle the best?
- How do you reduce stress and try to achieve balance in your life?
- How did you handle a request to do something contrary to your moral code or business ethics?
- What was the result the last time you tried to sell your idea to others?
- Why did you apply to our organization and what do you know about us?
- What do you think are advantages/disadvantages of joining our organization?
- What is the most important thing you are looking for in an employer?
- What were some of the common characteristics of your past supervisors?
- What characteristics do you think a person would need to have to work effectively in our company with its policies of staying ahead of the competition?
- What courses did you like best/least? Why?

- What did you learn or gain from your part-time/summer/co-op/internship experiences?
- What are your plans for further studies?
- Why are your grades low?
- How do you spend your spare time?
- If I asked your friends to describe you, what do you think they would say?
- What frustrates you the most?
- When were you last angry at work and what was the outcome?
- What things could you do to increase your overall effectiveness?
- What was the toughest decision you had to make in the last year? Why was it difficult?
- Why haven't you found a job yet?
- You don't seem to have any experience in __ (e.g., sales, fundraising, bookkeeping), do you?
- Why should I hire you?

A suggested guideline for your responses is as follows:

- Take about 70 seconds to state your qualification and give an example of it by explaining what, when, where and how you used it and what the successful outcome was.
- Take about 20 seconds to restate the qualification and outline the benefits transferable to the interviewer's organization.

For example, in response to the query, "What experience do you have organizing projects?" you would determine that the qualification being evaluated is organizational skills. Your Skill/Knowledge/Ability Statement could be, "I have developed excellent organizational skills by working on two major projects. The one I would like to tell you about came to a successful conclusion six months ago."

Whatever statement you make must be true! Don't lie or embellish. The illustration you would choose to confirm your statement would be a project that required similar competency to the typical project the prospective employer would want you to organize. Describe the what, who, when, where, why and how and talk about the successful outcome or what you learned from the experience. As you tell the story the employer can see or live through the action with you.

The next step is the one that most candidates for a position do not include. Tell the interviewer what benefits or competitive advantage you can bring to the position because of that experience. "As part of the team being formed, I would be able to coordinate ...." The key intention should be to sell yourself by using the story to support your strengths.

To supplement information obtained prior to the interview, you need to ask additional questions during the interview. Some questions will arise naturally throughout the interview but it is wise to bring some written questions with you. It shows the interviewer that you prepared for the interview by doing your homework. The questions should be pertinent to the position and show your enthusiasm and knowledge. By asking intelligent, well-thought-out questions you show the employer you are serious about the organization and need more information. If a question has been answered during the interview, do not ask it again. This will give the impression you are not listening. Here are some examples of questions you might ask:

- What do you see as the priorities for someone in this position?
- Would you be able to describe a typical day on the job? What would be a typical first-year assignment?
- What training programs do you have available for your employees?
- What level of responsibility could I expect in this position?
- Is there a typical career path for a person in this position?
- How are employees evaluated and promoted? What is a realistic time frame for promotion?

- Does the company have a promotion-from-within policy?
- What are the company's plans for the future? What do you see as the greatest threat to the organization?
- What/where are the greatest opportunities for the organization?
- How would you describe your organization's management style and working environment?
- What do you like most about your organization?
- Why is this position available? (Is it a new job or where did the former occupant go?)

Here are some tips for effective interviewing:

- Get a good night's sleep before your interview.
- Be punctual. Arrive 15 minutes early to allow yourself time to collect your thoughts. Take the opportunity to observe the working environment. Keep your eyes and ears open. Be friendly with everyone.
- Try to get the interviewer to describe the position and duties to you early in the interview so that you can relate your background and skills to the particular position.
- Give descriptive examples or proof whenever you can throughout the interview. The true stories you tell about yourself will differentiate you from the other applicants.
- Watch the interviewer for clues on how the interview is progressing. Is the interviewer's face or body language telling you that your answers are too long, not detailed enough, too boring, etc.? If in doubt, ask the interviewer if more or fewer details are needed.
- Listen carefully to the question and the way it is phrased.
- If it can be interpreted in more than one way and if you are unsure what the interviewer really wants you to discuss, ask for clarification.
- If the interviewer becomes silent, look for the reason. Has the person momentarily run out of questions? Is the person testing you to

see how comfortable you are with silence? Is the interviewer finding your answers too brief and waiting for you to elaborate more in order to get a better sense of who you are?

- When the interviewer asks about your weaknesses, choose something work-related but not so serious as to disqualify you. Briefly mention one weakness and then show what you have learned from the experience or what you are doing to change. If pressed for more than one weakness, have another one or two ready to discuss. You can also take a strength and use it as a weakness. I am a perfectionist. I get too involved in my work and then say how you compensate for this 'weakness.'
- If you are asked about any negative employment experience (e.g., being fired, trouble with supervisor), don't criticize past employers. Briefly acknowledge any difficulty and say what you have learned or discuss the positive outcome of the situation.

Do note there are clear human rights guidelines for employment interview questions. Applicants for employment may be asked to divulge only information that has relevance to the position applied for. Employers, by law, must focus on gathering relevant information in order to decide if the applicant is able to perform the functions of the position.

Some employers erroneously believe that they have a right to ask any question they choose since they are paying the salary. Others are simply awkward in their technique and an unlawful question results. Human rights law, however, does not distinguish between the interviewer who is asking questions with the intent to discriminate and the one who is just curious or inept at interviewing.

There are questions that are appropriate and questions that are illegal. You do not have to answer questions that are illegal. Since 1962, the Ontario Human Rights Code has been a model for employment practices. The code prohibits discrimination in employment on the grounds of:

- Race

- Ancestry, place of origin
- Color
- Ethnic origin/citizenship
- Creed
- Sex
- Sexual orientation
- Age
- Record of offences
- Marital status
- Family status
- Disability

Although it is ultimately the responsibility of the interviewer to know the law, this may not always be the case. It is to your advantage to be informed on the subject.

You've done the reading and know your rights as they pertain to the interview. Now you're in the middle of one and have just been asked what is clearly an illegal question. What should you do? There is no clear-cut answer. Much depends on you.

In some cases you may be able to answer the "hidden" question. Try to think of what information the employer is trying to elicit. Example: "Do you have or plan to have children?" may be a disguise for "Are you going to be able to work overtime?" or "Will you be requesting time off for school holidays/events?" In this example, your answer should convey your willingness to work overtime as required or make alternate child care arrangements.

You may elect to say "Why do you ask?" or "Would you explain how this point is connected to the qualifications for this job?" This may cause the employer to reconsider and/or clarify the question. This may offend some employers but probably not the majority.

If you feel that you should not answer the question (you shouldn't have to, after all) or that you are not interested in working for the company, you may state, "I don't feel obligated to answer that" or "That question is inappropriate." If you choose this option you will either enlighten (the employer may not realize it is illegal and will be happy that you pointed it out) or offend (the employer may not consider you for the position). Don't inquire about salary, bonuses or benefits in the initial interview. If you are pressed to give a salary expectation, turn it around to the interviewer and ask what the organization would ordinarily pay a person with your credentials. If you are still pressed, know what salary range would apply to that type of job in that geographic location. Try to obtain this information by speaking to people in the field prior to your interview or look it up online.

Practice in a mock interview with another person. Check for quality of information in your answers and the positive, nonverbal reinforcement of your words. By speaking out loud you can "hear" your answers to be sure you cover the topic well. Don't practice so much that you lose your spontaneity and your answers sound rehearsed.

If you do not receive a job offer (especially if you felt the "fit" was very good), you may want to contact the interviewer to get feedback on your performance. It could be (1) they hired someone with better qualifications, or (2) you didn't adequately present your qualifications, thereby causing an incorrect assessment of your capability. If the reason is (1), keep going ... you'll find the right match! If the reason is (2), learn from this and make the necessary changes in your next interview!

Mid-Life Career Changing in the New Economy

Individuals changing careers in mid-life need to analyze and understand the problem of "Ageism," how age discrimination affects their job search and most importantly, what they can do to empower themselves and find meaningful work in this difficult job market.

Marc Freedman, author of *The Big Shift: Navigating the New Stage beyond Mid Life* writes: "Thirty-year retirements in the era of the Great Recession? Let's face it. That is simply not going to work, nor is it desirable. Tough economic times and an aging population are changing how we approach retirement. Never before have so many people had so much experience and the time and the capacity to do something significant with it. The result is a realization that, though problems like "Ageism" are real, the potential for Mid-Life workers to contribute and THRIVE in the new workforce is also very real!"

Here are some popular myths about Ageism that are in conflict with the existing reality:

Myth: *"If you don't get a job and you are older it must be age discrimination."*

Reality: Job seekers often make mistakes in their job search long before ageism can occur.

Example: Employers scan résumés for 5-10 seconds. Résum not targeted are discarded.

Myth: *"Older workers are always discriminated against."*

Reality: Age is still an asset. Most companies still appreciate experience. Most teams still have older workers on them.

Example: Companies like Weyerhaeuser, Boeing and Home Depot actually have programs in place to retain and hire older workers. Like all job seekers, it is best for older workers to focus on "company cultures," NOT "job titles." You will probably not be happy working for a company that does not share your values. See: http://www.aarp.org/work/employee-benefits/best_employers/ .

Myth: *"Age discrimination is always about 'AGE.'"*

Reality: Ageism is often a euphemism for other concerns: Employers are often "afraid" that:

- You will not be adaptable.
- You will not be manageable.
- You will not be good with technology.
- You are overqualified and you will "jump ship."

The trick is to address these specific fears. Targeted cover letters, résum and interview answers that show you as adaptable, team-oriented and good with technology often eliminate age discrimination at its roots.

Myth: *"'The Wage/Age Dilemma'— Employers save money by paying younger workers less. "*

Reality: Older workers often need less training and have the experience to do the job better and faster.

Myth: *"You have to be 'old' to suffer from Ageism."*

Reality: Age is relative and can be used as a basis for discrimination against both "young" and "old."

Myth: *"Older people are not respected in our society."*

Reality: Recent studies show that the United States is one of the least ageist societies.

Myth: *"Older workers cost more money through lost time and health care expenses."*

Reality: Younger workers tend to still have children at home which results in more lost time and health care expenses. They also have more accident-related injuries that result in longer time out.

To read the Age Discrimination in Employment Act of 1975, go to: http://www.dol.gov/oasam/regs/statutes/age_act.htm.

Age discrimination shares similarities with other forms of negative discrimination like racism and sexism.

Stereotypes about populations make it difficult to see real individual people. Finding a job is all about your personal story. You will not find meaningful work if your personal story is stifled by stereotypes and generalizations. Ageism is possible in each phase of a job search. Age discrimination can creep into cover letters, résumés, interviews and the hiring process.

Here are some basic tricks for avoiding these pitfalls:

- Play to your strengths.
- Alleviate employers' fears.
- Take out information you do not need or that will obviously "date" you. (Be cautious!)

Ask Yourself:

- How is the movement against Age Discrimination like other movements against injustice?
- What can I do to overcome Ageism and find meaningful work?

Here is a 10-step method for combating Ageism and turning 'age' into an asset:

1. Make space for yourself. Balance your emotions. Emotions drive our job search. Therefore success in any job search is inseparably connected with the emotions of the job seeker. This is especially true when it comes to mid-life career changes. Positive and energetic job seekers find work faster than those who dwell on their problems. Yet we all have negative feelings when we are unemployed. So what can we do?

HEALTH: Doctors will tell you there are two things that are linked to ALL health issues: diet and exercise. Small changes here provide a stronger emotional base to work from.

HAPPINESS: When you start to feel depressed, desperate or insecure, take a break from your job search and do something you love. Seek out positive things.

ACTION: When you return to your job search, do not fixate on the problems at hand. Start to look for specific solutions!

Get help with finances:

- You paid taxes so that support systems are in place to help you when you are unemployed. Use them. Government programs, unemployment, public assistance and community organizations offer temporary relief. Go to http://www.seakingwdc.org/workforce/older-workers.html
- Tools like the Self -Sufficiency calculator are there to help you balance your budget and also to find financial resources. http://www.thecalculator.org

Take advantage of this "Cross Roads" moment:

- Successful mid-life career changers have a "Gap Year" between jobs that helps amplify perspective.
- "Liminality" is as important as "structure" in our lives. (In anthropology, liminality, from the Latin word *limen*, meaning "a threshold.")

2. Practice self-reflexivity. Many find it hard to be 'self-reflexive' (navel gazing). After 20 years in one career it can be hard to see options. Ask yourself what do I do for fun? What really makes me happy? What have I enjoyed the most out of all the jobs I have held? Use career coaches, career guidance tools and advice from people you trust to help determine who you really are and what your real strengths are. Passion + interest + abilities = meaningful work.

3. Develop Your Brand. To be happy at work we have to have passion. Passion comes from knowing our personal story. The unique combination of transferable skills, values, interests and abilities that we possess is our story. It is our BRAND.

Your brand should be:

S - imple

A - ppropriate

M - emorable

If you do not take your Brand seriously, no one else will. Develop a 30-second commercial (elevator speech). Answer the question: "How are others seeing me?" Adapt your message to the audience at hand. Use your brand to specifically combat Ageism.

4. Know your market. Your Brand will connect with certain companies and not with others. Compare REI (stewardship, community, sustainability operations) and Boeing (leadership, integrity, quality). They have different values they focus on. You can only find this out by research. Why waste time with organizations that do not share your values? There are actually shortages in many career fields! Understand "in demand" jobs, eligible training programs and funding options. Go to: http://www.careerbridge.wa.gov/

5. Establish a job plan. Attend job search workshops. Three strategies for success in combating Ageism and growing your Brand are: Be a "Solution focused," "Systems thinker" who "adds value." Improvise, adapt and overcome. Try to look at things from different angles. Go to:

http://www.stolaf.edu/services/cel/Alumni/Your_Path_to_Success.pdf ('Flow Chart' article in the *US News and World Report*)

6. Establish and LIVE a networking strategy. Attend workshops about effective networking for the new economy workshop. Use your wealth of knowledge, experience and contacts to your advantage! Networking allows you to become an individual again ... let them see you and not some stereotype. Remember: "People Hire People They Know!"

7. Use technology and keep learning. The point is not to try to "appear young" or become a "slave to technology." The point is to leverage tools to your advantage. Social networking sites such as www.linkedin.com can serve as a hub to continue to build your brand. (Notice that this is step 7 and not step number 1.)

8. Anticipate problems and seek solutions before you need them. Finding a job is a FULL TIME job and probably the toughest job you will ever have. Successful people spend most of their time in preparation. If you are busying yourself with research, learning about your industry, growing your Brand and networking, you will notice obstacles in your path long before you get to them. Amplify your perspective and you will find meaningful work.

9. Help others, be open for advice and volunteer! The best networkers help others. If you are active in your community and industry and open to new ideas, people will take notice. Volunteering, AmeriCorps, affinity groups, job clubs and so on are not just for first-time job seekers any more.

10. STAY RELEVANT! Set the pace for others to follow. Consider how you can add value to everything you do. Notice trends, accept change, follow movements that you believe in. Remember: The new movement is toward an acceptance of the true value of the "Encore Years." Mid-life can be the time when all your skills, experience and passion reach their highest potential!

Suggested Reading List and Helpful Resources:

Books:

The Big Shift: Navigating the New Stage beyond Mid-Life, Marc Freedman

Your Next Career: Do What You've Always Wanted to Do, Gail Geary

Finding Your Very Next Best Work Life: Strategies for Successful Career Change, Martha Mangelsdorf

Guerrilla Marketing for Job Seekers, Jay Levinson and David Perry

Internet Resources:

Need help with basic job search skills? (e.g., Creating a Job Plan, Résumés, Interviewing, Networking)

http://worksource.southseattle.edu/jobs.aspx

http://www.kcls.org/learning/careers/

Proof that employers NEED older workers:

http://www.employexperience.com/

"Developing the Workforce as It Matures." Emerging Models and Lessons from the Mid-point of the Aging Worker Initiative

http://www.compete.org/publications/detail/1679/developing-the-workforce-as-it -matures/

Bridging the Skills Gap: Why Mature Workers Matter–by Council for Adult and Experiential Learning (CAEL) and the Council on Competitiveness, 2009. http://www.cael.org/pdfs/116_bridgingtheskillsgap

Regional Economic and Workforce Strategies: A Focus on the Mature Workforce New Opportunities for Meeting Skill Needs - by the Council for Adult and Experiential Learning (CAEL) and the Council on Competitiveness, 2009 http://www.cael.org/pdfs/115_regionaleconomicandworkforcestrategies_final.

Timing of Retirement and the Current Economic Crisis. by the Sloan Center on Aging & Work at Boston College, Fact Sheet, August 2009 http://www.bc.edu/content/dam/files/research_sites/agingandwork/pdf/publications/FS25_TimingofRetirement.pdf

The "New Unemployables": Older Job Seekers Struggle to Find Work During the Great Recession. Comparing the Job Search, Financial and Emotional Experiences of Older and Younger Unemployed Americans - by Maria Heidkamp, Nicole Corre, and Carl E. Van Horn. The Sloan Center on Aging & Work at Boston College, Issue Brief, http://www.bc.edu/research/agingandwork/archive_pubs/IB25.html

The job market is constantly changing. Although you will encounter obstacles and challenges that were never there before, you will also find new resources and opportunities that were previously unavailable. Whatever situation you find yourself in, your best chance for using it to your advantage lies in staying current with changes as they occur.

CHAPTER 12 : TAKE ADVANTAGE OF TODAY'S TOOLS

Internet 101: The Basics

The Internet is a dazzling information resource providing access to individuals, companies and organizations from around the world. There are thousands of career and job search sites on the web. The powerful and dynamic technology of the internet can enhance your job search activities in many ways. You can:

- Collect data online in a relatively short amount of time instead of spending hours, days, or weeks in the library gathering bits and pieces of information from many sources.
- Conduct your job search research anytime that fits your schedule even if it's two o'clock in the morning. The internet remains open 24 hours a day, long after libraries and career centers are closed for the night.

Here are a few things you can do on the internet to enhance your job search:

- Visit company websites.
- Get the latest stock market reports and financial information.
- Search for newspapers, trade publications, books, and articles.
- Tour cities you may be considering for relocation.
- Obtain salary surveys and read about job market projections.
- Research hundreds of industries and professions.
- Network with potential employers and other job seekers.
- Submit online résumés and participate in electronic interviews.

Some internet job-search resources you may find helpful are:

- *America's Top Internet Job Sites*
- *Career X Roads: Directory of Job, Résumé, and Career Management Sites on the Web*
- *The Directory of Websites for International Jobs*
- *The Guide to Internet Job Searching*
- *Job-Hunting on the Internet*
- *Recent Graduate Web Sites*

You should become familiar with these popular search engines:

- www.google.com
- www.yahoo.com
- www.ask.com

LinkedIn 101

Where can you showcase your skills and talent, connect with over 100 million professionals (and growing), control your online brand, learn about industry news, join groups and be found and pursued for job opportunities that are relevant to you? The answer to all these questions is LinkedIn. Are you linked in?

If you do not currently have a FREE profile on the professional social networking site with LinkedIn, what are you waiting for? Setting up your profile is easy because the site is very user-friendly and many of the features will be familiar to you if you are acquainted with Facebook or Twitter. For example, you can post statuses on LinkedIn about what you are working on or even link your Twitter account to LinkedIn to update automatically. You can also "follow" companies in a way that is similar to following your favorite celebrity on Twitter. If you need further help getting started beyond the instructions below, check out this link for a short tutorial: http://learn.linkedin.com/what-is-linkedin/.

Step 1: Provide your first and last name, email and set up your password.

Step 2: Fill in your professional profile information. Feel free to reference your résumé for the content but realize that your profile should not be an exact replica of your résumé. Aim to use less than 2000 words and, unlike a regular résumé, it is OK to use the word "I." This is the next-generation of your professional credentials. Here is a brief overview of some of the main sections:

- Photo: Your profile will not be complete until you add your picture. This helps people quickly identify and remember you. Make sure the photo you select is a professional- looking headshot.
- Summary: Your 30-second commercial. Summarize your experience, goals, background and interests in an impactful way that will engage the reader. Use your dependable strength report if you have one.
- Professional Experience: Remember to use clear and concise accomplishment-oriented statements that highlight your dependable strengths. Tell a story that highlights the role you played in making successful projects happen and tell what the outcome was.
- Recommendations: This is the perfect place to collect and display endorsements from your supervisors, professors and coworkers. This will lend credibility to your work and showcase why people love working with you.

Step 3: Start connecting with colleagues and friends. You will be astonished to see how many people you know are already on LinkedIn. You can search by your previous schools or places of employment and also import your email contacts. Now you are ready to send a message to a user if you are connected or an "inMail" if you aren't but wish to be introduced. Networking is critical to your career success!

Step 4: Start leveraging LinkedIn's resources to benefit your career! You can download the app to your iPhone or Android device to continue networking when you are on the go. Always be sure that your information is up-to-date.

Why should you join LinkedIn?

- It shows that you are plugged into the latest technology.
- Your "Public Profile" will be shown to users not registered on LinkedIn who are "Googling" you; therefore you are controlling the information you WANT them to see. You can also personalize a "Vanity URL," which provides you with a custom web address for promoting your profile. This URL is part of your personal branding and can be included on résumés, business cards, email signatures, blogs, and portfolios.
- You can research companies or perform blind "reverse" company reference checks. Companies will typically check your references but have you ever thought to check theirs? You can also use this feature to look up the people you are going to be interviewing with or gauge the health of the company by scrutinizing the rate of turnover. Furthermore, once you have the job, you can look up
- your fellow-employees' profiles to get to know them faster.

There are many more advanced tools and uses for LinkedIn. You should explore it on your own or look for workshops that offer further tips on how to use LinkedIn in your job search. A word of warning! It is important to be aware of your online presence while using online networking tools. Your contact information should be accurate but make sure that you do not have information or content online that you wouldn't want a potential employer to see. Clean up your online identity by setting accounts on social networking sites to private and/or removing questionable material such as blog entries, photos, quotes, comments and applications. Be sure to present a positive image to those who may be looking at your online profiles. You may want to Google your name to see what results are generated and adjust your privacy settings on the sites accordingly.

You can monitor your online presence on sites such as Namecheck.com. Remember, your online presence conveys who you are—make sure you are projecting a professional brand. Be careful that your online image is true to who you are but does not disclose so much personal information that you risk identity theft or possibly scaring off potential employers.

You can increase your professional online presence by keeping up-to-date in your area of interest and finding blogs and articles of interest. Write and submit articles on relevant blogging sites in order to create dialog, demonstrate your area of expertise, and establish your professional image or brand. You can also create your own blog on sites such as SquareSpace.com (starting around $13 per month) or use Wordpress.com. On these sites you can quickly set up your website and create your own personal brand. A good resource to utilize to find out more about this topic is *How to Find a Job on LinkedIn, Facebook, Twitter and Other Social Networks,* by Brad and Debra Schepp.

Applying for Jobs Online

Federal regulations from the Office of Federal Contract Compliance Programs (OFCCP) now require many employers to collect and track Equal Employment Opportunity data for all applicants. Due to logistical complications and sheer volume, many employers are now only able to accept applications via their websites, which allows them to take advantage of their centralized applicant tracking systems. While this may appear (and actually be!) cumbersome to job applicants, you must carefully follow employer instructions if you want to be considered. So don't necessarily interpret an employer's mandate to "go to our website" or "apply online" as disinterest; it's most often simply a company's policy developed to meet federal requirements and is being fairly and consistently applied to all applicants.

So why even meet with employers in person nowadays? Job fairs and other networking events still offer great opportunities to sell yourself in person, learn about the company and their opportunities, ask key questions that can help with the online application process (e.g., What résumé format works best with your system? What skills does your company value most? When should I follow up? What department has current/anticipated openings?), and face-to-face interaction gives you an advantage.

So you've been instructed to apply through the company's website. How do you make your résumé stand out? Here are some tips that may be helpful:

- Use key words. Many employers utilize candidate contact management systems that allow for keyword searches (a good reason to include key course titles and skills sections) so use the words/language in the job ad as your model.
- Be thorough, follow directions and proofread. Enter correct data in the correct fields; complete all fields, even those that aren't required (including any optional assessment tests); spell and grammar check, if possible.
- Tailor the application. As with all aspects of the job search, you're most effective if you tailor your information to the position.
- Make comments. Many online applications have a catch-all section of this sort; use it to include information you're unable to include elsewhere (e,g., a skills inventory, professional organization involvement, remarks that show you've researched the company/industry).
- Follow up. Email or call the recruiter after completing the online application.

Organizing and Tracking Your Job Search

When conducting a job search, it is important to be organized. Use a journal or table to track where you found a job posting, whom you called, emailed, met at a networking event, whether they replied back or whether they supplied you with a lead to someone else. Here is a sample record sheet that you can set up in Microsoft Excel. It will help you to stay focused.

SAMPLE RECORD SHEET

			Type of Contact (and Date)				
Organization	Address/ Phone	Contact person	Website	Resource	Interview	Email/ Phone	Action needed

By doing your homework, researching various labor markets and career paths, doing informational interviews and possibly volunteering, you will start eliminating opportunities that are not right for you and begin focusing on just two or three career paths. This entails goal setting, decision-making, and action planning. And goal setting is being clear about what you want. When you know what your goals are, you must write them down. Motivational speaker Zig Ziglar once said: "Goal setting is bringing the future into the present so you can do something about it now."

6 Steps to Finding Your Next Job

There are no secrets to a successful job search but there are a series of steps you need to take to make your search a winning one. Following these steps will increase your chances of finding a more satisfying job in a shorter amount of time.

Step 1–Know Yourself. Conduct a thorough self-assessment to determine your skills, abilities and interests. Know your skills and what you have to offer an employer. You will need to be able to articulate your skills and abilities both in writing (your résumé and other job search tools) and in speaking (the interview).

Step 2–Know the Job Market. Do you know how the job market operates and screens people? How are people generally hired in the field you are interested in? What companies exist? What are they like? Who is hiring?

Step 3–Know what you are looking for. Although it is useful to remain open to unexpected opportunities, your job search will be an easier one if you have a focus. Learn more about specific jobs. What do people actually do in these jobs? What might be a good match for you?

Step 4–Develop job search tools. To facilitate your job search you will need an up-to-date résumé that really speaks to employers. You will need to know how to write good cover letters, thank you notes, and how to fill out applications to your best advantage.

Step 5–Use a systematic search method. Organize your job search as if it were a full-time job! Structure you time effectively and keep track of all your activities. Try to stay positive.

Step 6–Develop good interviewing skills. Although a good résumé might get you in the door, it's the interview that will get you the job. Learn the best techniques and keep interviewing until you hear those magic words: Congratulations, you're hired!

The pyramid below graphically illustrates the job search process:

Job Quest Process

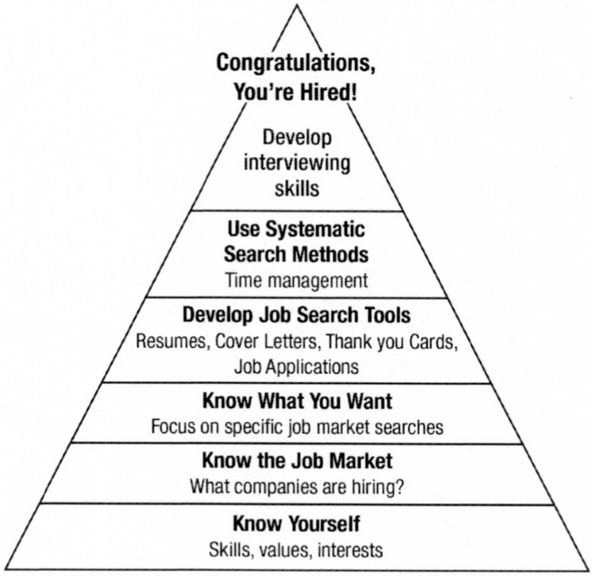

6 Steps to Fulfilling Work

As you move forward on your path toward your ideal career, here are some key points to keep in mind:

1. Define what fulfillment means to you. Only you know from your deepest core what a fulfilled life looks like. When you hear the word fulfillment, what do you imagine? Write down your vision of a fulfilled work life. What elements does it include (power, money, fame, autonomy, independence, learning, etc.)?

2. Identify your talents. You do some things naturally well and sometimes these things come so easy to you that you don't recognize them as your unique strengths. So let's identify yours:

- Yearnings can reveal your talents especially those you felt early in life. Consider the activities you naturally felt drawn to as a young person. Which ones continue to whisper to you over the years?
- Things you learn easily are a sign of where your talents lie. Take a moment to think about what you learn easily.

3. A clue is found in what satisfies you. If it feels good when you're performing an activity, you're probably using one of your natural strengths.

4. Once you have your vision and have acknowledged your talents,put some energy behind it. Write your vision in the present tense as if you already have it. Be able to see and feel your perfect workday. Keep it in front of you where you can read it 20 times a day!

5. Set a foundation under your dreams. If you want to get from where you are to where you want to go, you have to have a plan. Write out your desires, be clear, be specific, be able to measure it and set a time that you'll complete each step (see Setting SMART Goals.)

6. Have a strategy to deal with your "yes, buts." What do your "yes, buts" say when you think about living your life with fulfilling work? So what do you do with them?

a) Listen to their objections. Catch yourself when you're worrying. Make a list of your own personal "yes, buts."

b) Number your list. Which one pops up the most in your mind—your #1 "yes, but?"

c) When you notice one of your "yes, buts" crossing your mind, recognize it for what it is—"Oh, here comes one of my 'yes, buts' again." Before long, your "yes, buts" will loosen their power over you. Accept them; don't empower them.

Adapted from the work of Ann Ronan, PhD., http://authenticlifeinstitute.com/?tag=ann-ronan

The pyramid below provides a good illustration of the career quest process:

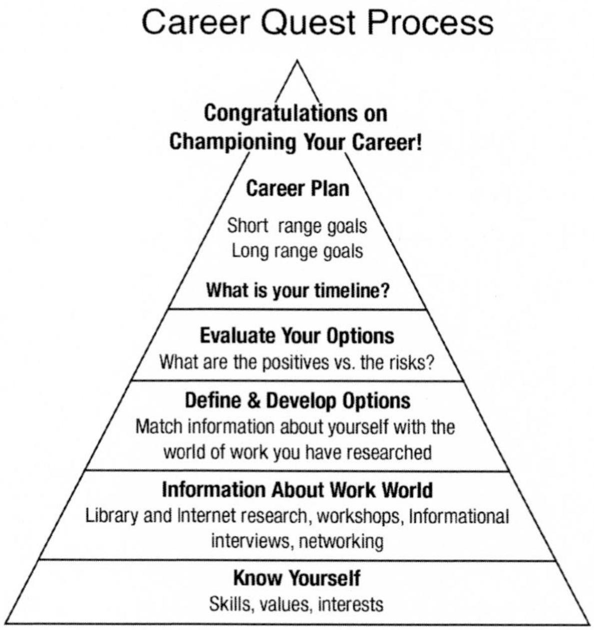

Above all, be kind and gentle with yourself in this process. Beating ourselves up for every minute failure or delay in meeting our goals is, of course, counterproductive. When we do meet challenges along the way, it is important to be objective and evaluate by asking relevant questions. "What happened?" and "What could I have done differently?" "What was the obstacle?" Maybe you set your goal too high. Reevaluate the goal and keep moving forward.

Ultimately our beliefs, coupled with appropriate actions, will keep us moving forward to our goals. You have to make your opportunities. You have to seek them out. You can't just sit there and wait for them to happen to you. Make that phone call, make the initial contact and put yourself out there. Just keep moving forward.

Good luck on championing your career!

APPENDIX

Since this book has been published in the Pacific Northwest, a number of the resources provided here are for that region; however, an effort has also been made to include many resources from highly reputable institutions in other regions. You should also consult the resources that are available in your own region from educational, non-profit and government institutions.

Once again, please note that, although the urls provided here were current at the time of publication of this book, urls change frequently so that some extra searching may be required to find the resource you are looking for.

Career Resources

from the University of South Florida Career Center

http://careerresource.coedu.usf.edu/selfassessment/selfassessment.htm

Self-Assessment

Florida Choices: https://secure.flchoices.org/ - State career information delivery system for high school students and adults that is free of charge for Florida residents. Contains an Interest Profiler and Work Values Sorter as well as information on occupations, schools and scholarships.

Self-Directed Search: http://www.self-directed-search.com/ - The SOS takes only 15-20 minutes to complete online. After your payment is verified, your personalized report will appear on your screen. Note: Paid site.

Career Key: http://www.careerkey.org/ - If you are a student, adult, parent, teacher or counselor, check out this Career Key by Dr. Lawrence Jones.

Michigan Occupational Information System: http://www.mivhs.org/Students/Career-Planning - Complete a brief but free career survey divided into areas of interests, aptitudes and experiences.

Kuder® Career Planning System: http://www.kuder.com/ Take the KUDER online and discover your career interests. Note: Paid site.

Career Planning Tests: http://www.actstudent.org/career/ or http://www.assessment.com/ Discover your ideal career! Career planning and career counseling (as well as career assessment) to help students and career changers identify and search for their ideal career.

O*NET Resource Center: http://www.onetcenter.org/ Contains various assessments including an Interest Profiler, Ability Profile, Work Importance and a Work Importance Locator.

The Princeton Review: http://www.princetonreview.com/ Provides a description of interests and work style.

Personality Assessment

The Kiersey Temperament Sorter II: http://www.keirsey.com/sorter/register.aspx Take this questionnaire to find out about your personality! It uses attributes of four temperaments to help people assess their preferences.

TechQuest 2000: http://www.math.unl.edu/%7Enmsi/tQ2/3index1.html Start thinking about career opportunities in math, science and technology. Provides a self-inventory and career path assessment

Irenemyers.com: http://www.irenemyers.com/ The focal point of this site is a concept called "Life/Work Motivators," which is referred to as "Archetypes of Calling." By proceeding through the site, you will go through a sample version and discover what some of your strong Motivators are and give names to them in a way that has a charge for you and engages your imagination. The insight that comes will add a new dimension to the way you know yourself. You can use your Life/Work Motivator patterns as a new compass, Also find out about training in facilitating Life/Work Motivators.

Other Assessment/Information on Assessment

Personality: Character and Temperament: http://www.keirsey.com/temperament_vs_character.aspx - This site is all about Dr. David Keirsey's research and books on personality and character.

American Psychological Association: http://www.apa.org/ - This brochure provides information on psychological assessments and on the importance of evaluations with regard specifically to a child's cultural background and language. Also included are suggestions to help assure parents of the use of appropriate psychological measurements.

APA Science FAQ: http://www.apa.org/science/programs/testing/find-tests.aspx - The APA Science Directorate answers hundreds of emails each year from persons trying to locate the right assessment tool or find more information about psychological evaluations. APA neither sells nor endorses assessment instruments but it does provide guidance in using available resources to find psychological measurements. Answers to frequently asked questions are provided here.

Buros Institute of Mental Measurement: http://buros.org/ - Provides information on thousands of assessment instruments.

MentalHelp.net: http://www.mentalhelp.net/ - Offers great information about mental health, personality and psychological assessment.

American Counseling Association: http://www.counseling.org/ Contains resources and books as well as information on upcoming conferences and events.

CACREP: Council for Accreditation for Counseling and Related Educational Programs: http://www.counseling.org/site/PageServer?pagename=cacrep - The CACREP website is provided as a service to students, educators and those interested in the helping professions.

Worklife's Career Mastery: http://careermastery.com/ - Emphasizes a self-help approach to personal career management with four assessment instruments designed to help improve a person's "current career environment." Note: Paid site.

Job Search Resources

From the Center for Career Connections at Bellevue College, Bellevue, Washington

- **Résumés and Cover letters:**

http://www.quintcareers.com/Web_resume_samples.html - A multitude of quality sample résumés. Download the PDF's and use as a guide to create your own.

http://www.guintcareers.com/resres.html - Lots of résumé-writing articles, worksheets and checklists.

- **Interviewing:**

http://www.best-job-interview.com - Great information on interviewing. Lots of job-specific advice.

- **Career & Employer Research:**

D&B Million Dollar Directory-Available through the public library system, The D&B database contains detailed information on over 1,600,000 North American organizations with at least $l Million in revenue and/or 20 employees. A great way to locate potential employers that may fit your background or aspirations.

http://www.bizjournals.com/bizbooks - Puget Sound Business Journal. Resource that includes many lists of companies for various industries and sectors. Follow companies for which you are interested in working.

https://www.google.com/alerts - Use Google alerts to follow companies for which you are interested in working. Read recent articles and pick up job search leads.

http://depts.bellevuecollege.edu/careers/connect-career-management-system/ - Bellevue College Connect! BC's career management system provides job/internship/volunteer postings as well as resources for your job search, such as résumé and cover letter guides.

http://www.bls.gov/ooh/ - The Department of Labor's Occupational Outlook. A wealth of information about careers and industry outlooks.

http://www.wois.org - Washington State career information system which has a wealth of information on careers and occupations, as well as assessment tools.

http://www.khake.com - One of the most comprehensive sites available for career research. This site offers information and links to nearly every occupation.

http://www.rileyguide.com - One of the major portals to career and employment research. Full of information regarding career research, job hunting, picking a career, and employment agencies.

- **Comprehensive Job-Search Engines:**

http://www.indeed.com OR http://www.simplyhired.com - These are the top two job search engines. They pull job postings from every job and career site in the country. Search them all at once! Save time by setting up automatic updates to "feed" new jobs that are of interest to your email inbox.

http://www.craigslist.org - Free classified advertisements. Lots of local jobs. Subscribe to RSS feeds to get updates on jobs of interest.

- **Networking & Informational Interviews:**

http://www.linkedin.com - This is the premier professional networking site. It is also great for company research. Use it to target companies and people in your field of expertise. This is the best place to locate and set up informational interviews.

http://www.iloveseattle.org - Site listing local professional associations and networking events. This is the best resource for locating local networking events. Be sure to check this out in other cities across the country.

http://www.spu.edu/depts/cdc/students/gethired/documents/InformationalInterviewChecklist.pdf - Download an informational interview checklist to impress your new contacts.

http://www.quintcareers.com/informationbackground.html - How do you conduct an informational interview? Here is a useful tutorial that will take about 30 minutes to read. Go through this tutorial and you will be prepared to be a networking pro!

- **Business Cards:**

http://www.vistaprint.com - Print 250 free business cards! Use this website for free and inexpensive business cards.

- **Salary Information:**

http://www.payscale.com - Excellent source of detailed salary information. Fill out a free salary profile for a unique understanding of your current market rate.

http://www.salary.com - One of the top salary tools on the web. Salary information for your region and for thousands of job titles. Each job includes a description. Also available are relocation and cost-of-living tools.

Online Job Sources

(from South Seattle Community College Career Center WorkSource)

Go2WorkSource.com. www.go2worksource.com - In addition to thousands of searchable local jobs, this site has a lot of resources and links for job seekers and employers. Additional sites like this one are also available in most states and cities.

The Seattle Times and Seattle Post-Intelligencer www.nwjobs.com - Both list all of their classified ads in a searchable database on this page. Good old-fashioned want ads from the local paper all together on a web page.

Craigslist.org www.craigslist.org - Local classifieds and forums where you can find jobs, housing, goods, services and local activities in most major cities.

Indeed.com www.indeed.com - is a search engine that pulls from job search sites, newspapers, associations and company career pages. Enter in your zip code and find jobs posted on a variety of sites.

Campus Point www.campuspoint.com/ is a place to find local part-time jobs, internships and full-time jobs for college students and recent graduates. Their free services can help you connect with unique local jobs and careers!

Idealist.org www.idealist.org - Looking to work for a nonprofit? Here is a place to find jobs, volunteer opportunities, organizations, groups, events and more.

Career Builder www.careerbuilder.com - is not only a job search engine, this site can also compare the salary levels of listings for jobs.

JobDango.com www.jobdango.com/ - This is an employment search engine offering jobs in Oregon and Washington.

Monster.com www.monster.com - currently has more than 370,000 jobs posted. The company has acquired JobTrak and now provides job and résumé databases for more than 1,000 college career centers.

Seattle Community College District www.seattlecolleges.edu/hr/ - They post their college jobs on this site; other community colleges throughout the US also have their own websites so be sure to check out your local colleges or any college you wish to apply to for their current job openings.

City of Seattle Jobs www.seattle.gov/personnel/employment/ - This is where to search if you are looking for employment with the city of Seattle.

King County Jobs www.metrokc.govljobs/AllJobs.html - Here is the starting place when looking for a job with Washington State's King County. Updated weekly!

State of Washington http://agency.governmentjobs.com/kingcounty/default.cfm - If you are looking for a job with the State of Washington, this is where to start!

USA Jobs www.usajobs.gov/ - The official job site of the US federal government.

Additionally check out your local state, county, city and college websites. They all list current career opportunities and are generally updated weekly.

THE JOB LIST

Mayor's Office for Senior Citizens, City of Seattle

Age 55+ Employment Resource Center

www.seattle.gov/seniors: seniors@seattle.gov

The following list of job search sites and additional information can be found at http://agingkingcounty.org/joblist_010814.pdf

www.thebeehive.org/jobs – The Beehive job board and skills

www.careers.wa.gov/ – State of Washington Jobs

www.evergreenaspaonline.org/job-announcements/ – American Society for Public Administration Job Board

Fortress.wa.gov/esd/worksource - Find a WorkSource

www.compasshousingalliance.org - Compass Housing Alliance

www.encore.org – Older workers job site

www.glassdoor.com – Glass Door

www.govjobstoday.com – Government Jobs Today (municipal job site)

www.hagelsearch.com – Executive placement for nonprofits

www.Indeed.com – Web crawler that locates jobs posted on all Pacific Northwest job boards

www.jfsseattle.org/careers.html – Jewish Family Services

www.jobaline.com – A bilingual, mobile-first jobs marketplace

www.jobbait.com/services – Job Bait

http://www.jobs4point0.com/ – Over 40 years old job site

www.kingcounty.gov/jobs.aspx – King County Jobs

www.linkedinpersonaltrainer.com/ - The LinkedIn Personal Trainer – Learn how to use LinkedIn

www.nowcc.org – Older Worker Career Center

www.retiredbrains.com – Retired executive job site

www.rewa.org – Refugee Women's Association

www.seattle.gov/jobs – City of Seattle jobs

www.seattlegoodwill.org – Seattle Goodwill Industries

www.usajobs.gov – the United States Government Job site

www.vocationvillage.com/seattle - nonprofit – Directory of all Seattle nonprofit organizations

www.washington.edu/admin/hr/job – University of Washington Jobs

www.workforce50.com – Workforce 50

www.AskTheHeadhunter.com

https://www.usajobs.gov/ - USA Jobs –Federal Government opportunities

THE JOB LIST (continued)

The following is a list of specialized or niche job boards. These may be useful if your line of work is narrow, specialized or not generally well-known. This list is posted as a general resource for your convenience.

HealthcareJobsite http://www.healthcarejobsite.com/ is for job seekers and employers in the Healthcare industry.

AbsolutelyHealthCare.com http://www.absolutelyhealthcare.com is a healthcare and medical job board.

HireFlyer http://www.HireFlyer.com is the top job search website solution online.

Ad rants http://www.adrants.com Advertising jobs from your favorite advertising website.

iCrunchData http://www.icrunchdata.com - Jobs in Big Data, Technology, Statistics, Cloud, Mobile, Software & Analytics.

All HealthcareJobs http://www.AllHealthcareJobs.com - For healthcare professionals.

All RetailJobs.com http://www.allretailjobs.com/ The #1 Job Board for the Retail Industry.

IT Job Pro http://www.ITJobPro.com

Authentic Jobs http://www.authenticjobs.com/ - Where companies and creative professionals meet to make a better web.

Joblux http://www.joblux.us - Luxury brands and retail careers network,

beautyJOBshop.com http://www.beautyJOBshop.com - North America's online venue for beauty, spa, salon and fashion jobs.

Manufacturing Jobs http://www.jobsinmfg.com

ClearanceJobs http://www.clearancejobs.com - Clearance Jobs is a secure job board focused on candidates with active or current US government security clearances.

JobsInTrucks.com http://www.jobsintrucks.com/ - A driver job board

Juju http://www.Juju.com is a job search engine not a job board. Juju's search results in links to employment sites on the Internet.

JOB POSSIBILITY GUIDE

This guide was created by brainstorming and aligning the six basic Holland Code categories with commonly designated fields of employment. Perusal of the guide will suggest many other job possibilities that you might not otherwise think of.

Realistic

ARTS/ENTERTAINMENT/MUSIC: museum technician, commercial artist, display worker, industrial designer, sound effects technician, sign painter, stringed instrument repairer, band instrument repairer, fitter, teleprompter, jeweler, weaver, knitter, drafter, art restorer

BUSINESS RELATIONS/OFFICE: office machine operator, postal clerk, shipping and receiving clerk, stock clerk, secretary, administrative assistant, word processer, computer programmer, file clerk, bill collector, repossessor, employee benefits approver, billing machine operator

COMMUNICATIONS: printing press operator, photoengraver, lithographic worker, photographic laboratory worker, motion picture projectionist, broadcast technician, radio operator, telephone communications technician, bookbinder, film processor, offset plate-maker, technician, telephone service, offset cameraperson

CONSTRUCTION: asbestos remover, insulation worker, bricklayer, carpenter, cement mason, construction laborer, electrician, floor covering installer, glazier, lather, marble setter, machinery operator, painter and paperhanger, plasterer, housepainter, plumber and pipefitter, roofer, sheet metal worker, stonemason, structural/ornamental and reinforcing iron worker, rigger, machine mover, building inspector, dry wall finisher, dry wall taper, electrical wirer, ship fitter

EDUCATION/SOCIAL SERVICE/SOCIAL SCIENCE: driving or flying instructor, massage practitioner, individual or group sports instructor, physical education teacher, vocational agriculture teacher, industrial arts teacher, vocational school teacher

ENGINEERING/SCIENCE/TECHNICAL: forester, cartographer, city planner, forestry aide, broadcast technician, engineering and science technician, food processing technician, tool designer, aerial photographer, cheese maker, taxidermist, recycling operator, water treatment plant operator, mechanical tester, engineer (aeronautical, civil, industrial, mechanical, metallurgical, agricultural, mining), airplane navigator, airplane pilot, electronic technician, wood technologist, engineering aide

FARMING/OUTDOOR/FORESTRY: farmer, tree surgeon, tree trimmer, landscaper: bee keeper, technician, gardener, plant health technician, plant "sitter:' diver, crop duster, water well driller, commercial flower producer, hunting and fishing guide, prospector, groundskeeper, blacksmith, parking meter collector, wildlife attendant, animal groomer, range manager, horticulturist, park naturalist, fish and game warden, zookeeper, nursery manager, naturalist, forester

HEALTH/MEDICINE: medical laboratory technologist, medical records administrator, x-ray technologist, pharmacist, veterinarian, occupational therapist, dental hygienist, dentist, physical therapist, medical laboratory worker, medical record technician, veterinary assistant, respiratory therapy technician, nurse (LPN), electrocardiograph technician, electroencephalograph technician, medical assistant, optometric assistant, occupational therapy assistant, physical therapy assistant, operating room technician, embalmer

HOSPITALITY/RECREATION/SPORTS: Lifeguard, karate instructor, physical fitness instructor, athlete

INDUSTRIAL/MACHINE/REPAIRERS/OPERATORS: safety supervisor, machine tool worker, set up worker, tool and die maker, instrument maker, assembler, auto painter, blacksmith, electro-operator, furniture upholsterer, inspector, power truck operator, stationary engineer, waste water treatment plant operator, telephone installer and repairer, air conditioning, heating/refrigeration mechanic, appliance repairer, auto body repairer, auto mechanic, boat motor mechanic, business machine repairer, form equipment mechanic, industrial machine repairer, instrument repairer, jewelry repairer, locksmith, maintenance electrician, motorcycle mechanic, piano and organ tuner and repairer, TV and radio service technician, truck and bus mechanic, vending machine mechanic, watch repairer, welder and oxygen arc cutter, airplane mechanic, kiln attendant, watch repairer, computer service technician, diesel mechanic, electric sign repairer

MANUFACTURING/CRAFTWORK: patternmaker, molder, core maker, inspector, millwright, sewing machine operator, dental technician, shoe repairer, watch repairer, clock maker, taxidermist, furniture refinisher, wood finisher, cabinetmaker, bookbinder, upholsterer, apparel presser, mapper, plant attendant, dressmaker, garment cutter, model maker, weaver, knitter

MARKETING AND SALES: auto parts salesperson, gasoline service station attendant, automobile sales worker, marketer.

SERVICE, PUBLIC/PERSONAL: building custodian, pest controller, cook and chef, private household worker, firefighter, mail carrier, telephone operator, beautician, bartender, animal trainer, caretaker, meat cutter, baker, appliance demonstrator, maid, postmaster, meter reader, manicurist, cafeteria worker, caterer, trash hauler, security guard, solid waste systems manager, attendant (hat check), highway patrol officer, detective, police officer, armed services officer

TRANSPORTATION: aircraft mechanic, auto mechanic, air traffic controller, flight engineer, pilot, copilot, brake operator, bridge and building worker, locomotive engineer, locomotive firer, telegrapher, telephone and tower worker, inter-city bus driver, local transit bus driver, local truck driver, long distance truck driver, parking attendant, taxi driver, locomotive conductor, station agent, chauffeur, driver's license examiner, delivery person, messenger, elevator operator, route driver, shuttle service driver

Conventional

ARTS/ENTERTAINMENT/MUSIC: film editor, film librarian, script reader

BUSINESS RELATIONS/OFFICE: accountant, bookkeeper, bank cashier, teller, data entry clerk, keypunch operator, office clerk, office manager, statistical clerk, quality control manager, payroll clerk, cashier, computer programmer, accountant (CPA), systems analyst, actuary, claim examiner, underwriter, credit official, purchasing agent, budget reviewer, financial analyst, cost estimator, bank examiner, tax expert, mortgage specialist, controller, credit investigator, escrow officer, estate planner, revenue agent, title examiner, stockbroker, trust officer, statistician, court reporter, IRS agent, tax auditor, receptionist, title and contract searcher, secretary, public stenographer, filing clerk, typist, legal secretary

COMMUNICATIONS: scientific illustrator, science information specialist, radio engineer, index editor, ground radio operator, estimator (book publishing), cryptanalyst, book editor, manuscript reader, handbook writer, service publication writer, rewriter, proofreader, copywriter, greeting card editor, editorial assistant, copyreader, communication center operator, radio dispatcher, telegrapher

CONSTRUCTION: crew scheduler

EDUCATION/SOCIAL SERVICE/SOCIAL SCIENCE: demographer, math/science teacher, health educator, business education teacher, library assistant, bookmobile librarian, financial aid counselor, eligibility worker, Braille transcriber

ENGINEERING/SCIENCE/TECHNICAL: drafter, surveyor, assayer, biological aide, research aide, mathematical technician, model maker, psychometrist, dietitian, statistician, cartographer

FARMING/OUTDOOR/FORESTRY: range manager, soil conservationist, park ranger, animal health technician, husbandry specialist, ecology technician, breeder, conservation officer, fire lookout

HEALTH/MEDICINE: laboratory assistant, respiratory therapy technician, dental assistant, hospital records clerk, optician, optical technician, cytotechnologist, hematology technologist, food inspector, histology technician, dietetic assistant, orthopedic assistant, ophthalmology technician, dental hygienist, pharmacist, audiologist, blood bank technologist, cytologist, biometrist, mortician, hospital admitting clerk, hospital librarian, medical secretary, medical records administrator

HOSPITALITY/RECREATION/SPORTS: caterer, recreation facility attendant, travel counselor

INDUSTRIAL/MACHINE/REPAIRERS/OPERATORS: printer, instruction manual writer, typesetter

MANUFACTURING/CRAFTWORK: production planner, inventory controller, trade or technical editor

MARKETING AND SALES: property appraiser, agricultural commodities inspector, pharmaceutical salesperson, appraiser, examiner (tariff and schedules), securities trader, market analyst, convention manager, merchandise manager

SERVICE, PUBLIC/PERSONAL: budget counselor, court clerk, answering service worker, license clerk, registrar, directory assistance operator, telephone operator

TRANSPORTATION: customs inspector, customs agent, traffic manager, safety program coordinator, station agent (railroad), driver's license examiner, dispatcher, reservations agent

Investigative

ARTS/ENTERTAINMENT/MUSIC: scriptwriter, gag writer, motion picture narrator, art critic, music critic, theater critic, book critic, comedy writer, picture editor, scientific photographer

BUSINESS RELATIONS/OFFICE: abstract writer, publisher, law clerk, law librarian, patent attorney, probate lawyer, real estate lawyer, literary agent, patent examiner, legal assistant

COMMUNICATIONS: technical writer, language interpreter, newspaper reporter, journal editor, biographer, collaborator, columnist, essayist, manager of news/special events/public affairs, news analyst, public lecturer, public relations director, freelance writer, translator, proposal writer, organization newsletter editor, book reviewer, commercial writer, specification writer

EDUCATION/SOCIAL SERVICE/SOCIAL SCIENCE: research assistant, social scientist, English teacher, anthropologist, economist, geographer, historian, political scientist, sociologist, archivist, librarian, genealogist, social psychologist, college professor, experimental psychologist, counseling psychologist

ENGINEERING/SCIENCE/TECHNICAL: statistician, job analyst, biostatistician, chemical engineer, electrical engineer, biomedical engineer, biophysicist, electronics technician, biologist, mathematician, physical scientist, experimental psychologist, scientific researcher, chemist, geologist, metallurgist, geophysicist, meteorologist, oceanographer, biochemist, soil scientist, physicist, zoologist, botanist, spectroscopist, entomologist, geneticist, inventor, airplane navigator, astronomer, food scientist, geographer, seismologist, environmental analyst, veterinarian

FARMING/OUTDOOR/FORESTRY: agronomist, forest ecologist, horticulturist, plant breeder, soil conservationist, animal breeder

HEALTH/MEDICINE: public health nurse, speech pathologist, medical librarian, physician, bacteriologist, endocrinologist, hospital pharmacist, internist, pathologist, dentist, pediatrician, optometrist, physician, medical technologist, surgeon, registered nurse, chiropractor, osteopathic physician, anesthesiologist, clinical psychologist, nurse practitioner, veterinarian, medical technologist, medical laboratory technician

HOSPITALITY/RECREATION/SPORTS: sports announcer, sports editor

MARKETING AND SALES: book seller, direct mail specialist, market research analyst, marketing researcher

SERVICE, PUBLIC/PERSONAL: detective, polygraph examiner

Artistic

ARTS/ENTERTAINMENT/MUSIC: interior decorator, theater stage manager, floral designer, composer, artist, entertainer, actor, musician, singer, dancer, clothes designer, costume designer, fashion model, sculptor, musical arranger, photographer, potter, film maker, makeup artist, scenic designer, portrait painter, fabric designer, art restorer, calligrapher, spinner, gift wrapper, pet photographer, fashion design sketcher, style consultant, choreographer, puppeteer, repairer and restorer of art pieces, greeting card designer, needlecraft worker, orchestra conductor, lyricist/composer, playwright, novelist, poet, short story writer, clown, magician, jewelry designer and maker

BUSINESS RELATIONS/OFFICE: advertising executive, art museum director, curator, cataloger, commercial artist, florist, antique dealer, advertising layout artist, decorating consultant, concert manager, store window designer, display designer, art director, creative director

COMMUNICATIONS: scientific illustrator, author, librarian, reporter, producer, illustrator, free-lance writer, media specialist, photographer, fashion reporter, TV and radio caster, TV and radio programmer, TV and radio promoter, voice-over performer, TV cameraperson, TV and radio announcer, children's book writer, screen writer, copywriter, critic, cartoonist, photojournalist, disc jockey, narrator

CONSTRUCTION: metal sculptor, historic house preservationist, hand carver

EDUCATION/SOCIAL SERVICE/SOCIAL SCIENCE: dancing teacher, sewing teacher, craft teacher, makeup application teacher, music librarian, music historian/recorder, art teacher, language teacher, music teacher, educational film maker, media specialist, dramatics coach, choral director, art or music therapist, English teacher

ENGINEERING/SCIENCE/TECHNICAL: model builder, graphic designer, sign letterer and designer, technical artist and illustrator, compositor, architect, landscape architect

FARMING/OUTDOOR/FORESTRY: landscape gardener, taxidermist, naturalist

HEALTH/MEDICINE: medical illustrator, medical photographer, occupational therapist, prosthetist technician, occupational therapist assistant, music therapist,

sports photographer

INDUSTRIAL/MACHINE/REPAIRERS/OPERATORS: Industrial designer, industrial photographer, engraver, typesetter, typographer, linotype operator, printmaker

MANUFACTURING/CRAFTWORK: drafter, leather craftsperson, weaver, wood craftsperson, dressmaker, glassblower, knitter, tailor, product designer, metal craftsperson, toy designer, game inventor

MARKETING AND SALES: music salesperson, artists' agent, literary agent

SERVICE, PUBLIC/PERSONAL: cake decorator, personal shopper, theatrical dresser, interpreter for the deaf

TRA**NSPORTATION:** flight attendant

Social

ARTS/ENTERTAINMENT/MUSIC: music instructor, dramatic coach, tour guide

BUSINESS RELATIONS/OFFICE: hotel front office clerk, receptionist, bank teller, customer relations expert, information giver, social secretary, industrial tour director, employee counselor

COMMUNICATIONS: page

EDUCATION/SOCIAL SERVICE/SOCIAL SCIENCE: teacher aide, caterer, dormitory director, homemaking skills teacher, adult education teacher, vocational/technical teacher, art therapist, music therapist, dance therapist, home demonstration agent, physical education teacher, religious education director, elementary teacher, teaching nun, home economics teacher, rehabilitation counselor, mortgage counselor, school psychologist, teacher of handicapped, community health educator, chemical dependency counselor, correspondence school instructor, director of religious activities, home economist, minister, rabbi, priest

ENGINEERING/SCIENCE/TECHNICAL: vocational training instructor

FARMING/OUTDOOR/FORESTRY: county agricultural agent, Four H-Club agent, extension service specialist

HEALTH/MEDICINE: public health nurse, registered nurse, hospital patient representative, medical social worker, recreational therapist, occupational therapist, physical therapist, physical therapy assistant, nurse (LPN), nursing aide/order1y, occupational therapy assistant

HOSPITALITY/RECREATION/SPORTS: restaurant manager, hostess, tour guide, travel counselor, usher, social director, physical fitness instructor, sports instructor (skating. swimming. skiing. etc.), ski patroller, caterer, camp counselor, recreation leader

SERVICE, PUBLIC/PERSONAL: social worker, parole officer, welfare worker, case aide, case worker, correction officer, residence counselor, employment counselor, hotel housekeeper, waitress/waiter, barber, beautician, child care assistant, bellhop, bell captain, foster parent, homemaker, domestic, wedding consultant, governess, paid companion, houseparent, travel companion, day care provider

TRANSPORTATION: flight attendant

Enterprising

ARTS/ENTERTAINMENT/MUSIC: museum director, museum education director, interior designer, art dealer, stage director, disc jockey, fashion show producer, entertainer's agent, fashion coordinator, TV show hostess, literary agent

BUSINESS RELATIONS/OFFICE: corporation lawyer, personnel worker, FBI special agent, florist dealer, Chamber of Commerce executive, department store manager, personnel consultant, director, employment manager, small business manager, banker, manager, public relations worker, industrial relations consultant, small business owner, business broker, business agent, training director, criminal lawyer, interviewer, bank officer, corporate community service director, women's style shop manager, receptionist, hotel/motel manager, beauty shop manager, food service manager, courtroom stenographer, credit manager, political campaign manager, press agent, funeral director, restaurant proprietor, personnel clerk, store detective, resort owner, fund raiser, apartment house manager, lobbyist, investment fund manager

COMMUNICATIONS: literary agent, publicity director, telephone solicitor, foreign correspondent, TV or radio announcer, legislative lobbyist, television producer, trainer in writing and speaking, news commentator .

CONSTRUCTION: building superintendent, apartment house manager, general contractor, sales representative (building equipment and supplies)

EDUCATION/SOCIAL SERVICE/SOCIAL SCIENCE: college student personnel worker, school principal, superintendent, vocational counselor, YWCA staff, guidance counselor, social science teacher, home economics teacher, business education teacher, college career planning and placement counselor, missionary, training director, program director

ENGINEERING/SCIENCE/TECHNICAL: industrial psychologist

FARMING/OUTDOOR/FORESTRY: extension agent, outdoor leader/guide, agricultural sales representative

HEALTH/MEDICINE: hospital administrator, food service administrator, embalmer, pharmacist, volunteer coordinator, natural foods salesperson, natural cosmetics salesperson, pharmaceutical salesperson, dental and medical equipment and supplies salesperson

HOSPITALITY/RECREATION/SPORTS: athletic director, playground director, recreation leader, professional athlete, coach/instructor, manager of recreation establishment, umpire, camp counselor, party/catering planner, convention planner, demonstrator, sports official

INDUSTRIAL/MACHINE/REPAIRERS/OPERATORS: sales representative (computer systems, industrial machinery, precision instruments)

MANUFACTURING/CRAFTWORK: production coordinator, salary and wage administrator

MARKETING AND SALES: buyer, purchasing agent, securities sales worker, property rental agent, insurance sales, real estate sales, life insurance agent, real estate agent, retailer, computer sales, manufacturer's representative, sales manager, department store sales clerk, wholesale trade sales worker, sales promoter, auctioneer, sales director, market researcher, sales support staff

SERVICE, PUBLIC/PERSONAL: child care center manager, public administrator, legislator, consumer protection agent, safety educator, elected official, army officer, police officer, highway patrol officer, waiter/waitress, funeral director, beautician, executive housekeeper, child care worker, consumer advocate, court bailiff, personal shopper, institutional beautician, personal hairdresser, make-up technician, estate planner

TRANSPORTATION: travel agent, reservation agent, travel bureau manager, traffic agent, guide, traffic clerk, club travel arranger

8 Tips for Finding a Job: Job-Search Quick Guide

Money and time can limit the jobs you should apply for. Start by creating a budget to determine how much money you realistically need to make to pay your expenses.

- Be conservative in your budget as unexpected expenses can often occur.
- Set a goal for your required wage: (Example: $12 per hour x 20 hours per week = $960 per month).

1) Time

Once you know how much money you need to make to live, calculate the number of hours you can spend each week on your job search. The more time you can allocate the better, but be realistic.

- Example: "I can spend two hours per day on my job search, which totals 14 hours per week."
- Block off regular parts of your day to devote to your job search.

2) Who are you?

Your personality and background will help determine where you will best fit and where you will be most successful. Often college career centers provide assistance and resources to help you understand who you are and determine the types of settings in which you would best fit.

- What are your passions, interests and values? What is exciting or meaningful to you?
- What knowledge, skills and abilities have you gained through work, internships, school or volunteering?

3) What do you want?

Take some time to think about the fields that interest you or fields in which you have experience.

- Based on who you are, what type of work do you want to do?
- At what type of organizations would you want to work? (i.e., large or small shop, public or private, etc.)

4) Focus on a Target

One of the most important parts of a job search is creating a target for your job search. Often job seekers are willing to take anything, however employers want to hire individuals with specific interests and relevant skills. Target the jobs that you want and for which you are qualified.

- Create a target list of industries and companies that might match what you are seeking.
- Make sure that your list includes at least 10 companies and that no more than a third of them are large corporations (e.g.,. Microsoft, Boeing, Amazon, Google, Starbucks). Smaller companies are much more likely to interview you and it is easier to speak with a hiring manager.
- It is okay to have more than one target. If your job search is not resulting in any job offers, you can change your focus to a new target.
- Here are some resources for creating a target list
- Connect! https://bellevue-csm.symplicity.com/students
- http://www.washjob.com This is a list of all the companies in the State of Washington.
- D&B Million Dollar Directory (available at the public library): The D&B directory has detailed information on over 1,600,000 North American organizations.
- LinkedIn or Google Search.

5) Research

Job searching is a research project. Once you have identified what your target is, spend time researching the companies and industry in which you are interested. Organizations want prospective employees to be prepared and to have done their homework on the company. Do as much research as you can in your job search. Research the companies on your list to be well-prepared for networking and interviews.

6) Look Good on Paper and Online

Before you launch your job search campaign, you need a good résumé. In addition to your traditional résumé, make sure any information about you online (e.g., Facebook, Twitter, MySpace, LinkedIn, your blog, etc.) contains appropriate content in case an employer tries to learn about you. Tailor your résumé to each specific job and change it for every target.

- Highlight your accomplishments and achievements, not just your work duties.
- Edit your résumé thoroughly and have someone else help you check grammar and spelling.

7) Network & Meet People

The majority of jobs are not found online. These jobs are discovered through networking.

- Make a list of all your connections and contact the ones working in your field of interest. If you do not know anyone working in your field of interest, contact the people who may know someone in your field of interest (Example: Accounting: contact and meet with all the accountants you know to get advice for your job search and learn about their company).
- After meeting with your contacts, ask for referrals to other people in your field.
- Carry your list of target companies with you and ask friends and connections if they can refer you to anybody who works at a company on your list.

- Nearly every field has a professional association or society with rich networking opportunities. They often offer discounted student memberships. Go to http://www.iloveseattle.org for a list of associations and societies in the Seattle area. Other cities have similar sites. Be sure to check them out.
- Volunteering is a great way to meet potential employers, build new skills and stay occupied. Go to http://www.idealist.org for a list of volunteer opportunities.

8) Online Job Information:

Online job searching can waste hours of time. To maximize your time in your job search, set up automatic updates on job search engines to "feed" new jobs that are of interest to your email inbox. You can usually choose to receive the updates as often as you want. Begin searching on the sites below. When your search pulls up a lot of interesting jobs, save the alert and have it sent to your email:

- http://depts.bellevuecollege.edu/careers/connect-career-management-system/ The Center for Career Connections at Bellevue College has a great job posting board called Connect! You can set up a "Search Agent" that will alert you to new job postings.
- https://twitter.com/BellevueCCC - Bellevue College also has a Twitter page with job-search tips and articles.
- http://www.lndeed.com or http://www.simplyhired.com are meta-search engines that "pull" jobs from all public job boards. Instead of going to Monster.com or CareerBuilder.com, use Indeed.com and SimplyHired.com which pull from both.
- http://www.craigslist.org Craigslist is a popular website for job searching. Once you find search criteria that pulls interesting jobs, look in the bottom right corner for an orange button that says "RSS feed." Click on it to sign up for email updates on your searches.

- Google alerts: use Google alerts to get up-to-date news on companies on your target list.

Center for Career Connections at Bellevue College, Bellevue, Washington

Web: http://bellevuecollege.edu/careers or http://www.bellevuecollege.edu/internships/

The Three Ps of Interviewing: Preparation, Practice, Presentation

Preparation:

Know the package you have to sell.

- Be able to talk about your skills and interests. Prepare a 60-second commercial and practice it many times! Answer the question, "What value can you add to the company?"
- Be able to describe your past work experiences in terms that relate to the position for which you're interviewing. This is true of paid work, volunteer, internship or other kind of experience.

Know the Employer .

Research the organization before your interview. Find answers to such questions as:

- How long has this organization been in business?
- What is the organization's stated mission?
- What products or service does the company manufacture/sell?

- Who are the company's competitors?
- How is it organized?
- Do they offer structured or unstructured training for new employees?
- How many plants/stores/outlets do they have and in what geographic location?
- What is the range of salary and benefits?

Where can you look for this information?

- On the organization's website.
- Annual reports/brochures published by the company.
- In the public library's business section.
- In business news: read the paper and other business journals.
- If you know someone who works at the company, talk with her/him.

Practice

- Attend an interview workshop.
- Make use of interactive interview software if available.
- Make up a list of questions you think the interviewer might ask and get a list of frequently asked questions (from Career Services). Practice answering them aloud.
- Have a friend or partner sit down and role-play the interview with you.
- Practice before a mirror or if you have access to a video camera, record yourself responding to questions.
- Pay attention to your attitude. It will affect your body language, eye contact and general demeanor. Avoid nervous habits like fiddling with jewelry or clothes.

Presentation

Dress

- Dress to match the standards of the workplace where you're interviewing: if possible, find out how the people in the company dress then match their style or upgrade it a half step. (Remember that Friday is casual dress day in many places and you should dress according to their Monday-Thursday code!)
- If you're not sure about the dress code, always err on the conservative side. It's better to be overdressed than underdressed for an interview.
- An employer is more likely to notice things that don't look right rather than things that do. Excessive jewelry, perfume/cologne or wild hairdos are more likely to be noticed in a negative way than a simple, conservative style.

Thank you notes

- As soon as you return home from your interview, sit down and write a thank you note to the people who interviewed you. Remind them of the job you were interviewed for and why you would be a good fit.
- Type it using business style. If the interview was particularly informal and friendly, you might handwrite it. An emailed thank you is acceptable but the old-fashioned hard copy is noticed more.

Why do companies choose not to hire a candidate? Do you see yourself in any of these?

- Poor or inappropriate personal appearance.
- Intolerant, strong prejudices.
- Negative criticism of past employer.
- Vague and/or sloppy application form; narrow field of skills; and/or lack of interest in acquiring more skills.

- Wants job only for a short time.
- Self-engrossed, overbearing, overly aggressive, or "know-it-all" attitude.
- Lack of interest and enthusiasm.
- Late for interview.
- Impolite.
- Inability to express self clearly.
- Knows and asks nothing about the company.
- Lack of evidence showing excellence of past performance.
- Failure to use good eye contact.
- Overemphasis on money, interested only in dollar offer.
- Apparently passive and indifferent.

Some General Tips

- Be yourself.
- Get off to a good start by arriving early.
- Express a sincere interest in and enthusiasm for the job.
- Always be polite and friendly to the receptionist! S/he may be part of the interview team!

Source: WorkSource at South Seattle Community College

Preparing for Your Interview: Will you fit in? (Are you going to add value to the team?)

Employers need to see that you will do a good job and be a dependable employee. The most important thing they are trying to discover in an interview conversation is if you will be a good member of their team.

The best teams share common values that allow them to have success. What are your values? (Remember, "values" have a strong link to emotions. Your "feelings" affect your job success.)

In your journal, write and complete the following sentences:

- I feel like the most important thing I can do in my career is …
- I do not like it when people on my team …
- I am the most happy at work when…
- If I could change something about my last job it would be…
- If I could create my own dream job I would be sure that everybody on my team was …

From your answers above, create a list of your strongest values:

Preparing for Your Interview: Research the Company

You will not have a good interview conversation with an employer if you do not know how and why you are the right person for their company and their team. You have to do research!

The easiest way to start your research is to visit the company's website. When researching their website, look for:

- Their mission statement. In your journal, write how their statement matches up with your own values? (Be sure to describe yourself using their words).
- The population they serve. Are these the people you want to work with? Why?
- What services they provide. Do you believe in what they do? How can you help them do it better?
- How long they have been in business and how successful are they?
- Who works at the company/organization? Why do you want to work with them?

Now analyze your statements in this and previous activity sheets. Compare those with what you know about the company you are going to interview for. What values does the company have? How do your values line up with theirs? Create a statement that summarizes your values and how they line up with the job you want.

Preparing for Your Interview: Breaking Down Transferable Skills

Think about previous positions you have held and the tasks you completed in those positions. In your journal, create a chart with two columns. Write the tasks you have done in the left column. In the right column, identify transferable skills that might be associated with those tasks. Two examples are provided here to help you get started.

TASK

Used computers

TRANSFERABLE SKILL(S)

Knowledge of computer software

Adaptable to new software

TASK

Answered phones

TRANSFERABLE SKILL(S)

Customer service

Ability to multitask

Task-oriented

Ability to prioritize

Your Interview: Your 30-Second Commercial

Your "Brand" is the essence of who you are related to the job you want. It is your unique story. One way to share your "Brand" is with a 30-second "Elevator Speech."

Elements of this "Elevator Speech" might include: who you are, your skills and interests, and why you should be hired. Most importantly, it should connect your "values" with the job you want.

Consider these questions and write the answers in your journal:

- What elements of your past experience come together in the job you want now?
- What is something memorable about you that directly relates to the job you want?
- What specific achievement summarizes who you are in relation to the job you want?

Now analyze your statements in this and previous activity sheets. Compare those with what you know about the company you are going to interview for. Create a 30-Second Elevator Speech that connects you with a job you want and answers the question: "Tell me about yourself."

Resources / Further Reading

Internet Resources

1. http://2young2retire.com/wp/
2. www.authentichappiness.com
3. http://authenticlifeinstitute.com/?tag=ann-ronan
4. http://personalexcellence.co/
5. http://recareerinc.com/certification/dr-richard-p-johnson.aspx
6. http://www.en.wikipedia.org/wiki/Holland_Codes
7. www.authentichappiness.com
8. www.careerbuilder.com
9. www.careerinfonet.com
10. www.careers.org
11. www.dependablestrengths.org
12. www.heidelberg.edu/.../jfuller/Deciding%20Handbook.pdf
13. www.online.onetcenter.org
14. http://www.retirementoptions.com
15. www.rileyguide.com
16. http://www.wiu.edu/advising/docs/Holland_Code.pdf
17. http://www.ncda.org/aws/NCDA/pt/sp/resources

Books

1. What Color is Your Parachute? – R. Boles
2. What Color is Your Parachute? For Retirement – R. Bolles & J. Nelson
3. Zen & the Art of Making a Living – L. Boldt
4. Personal Excellence: Be your Best Self, Live Your Best Life - Celestine Chua

5. Finding Your Perfect Work – Paul & Sarah Edwards
6. Creative Decision Making Using Positive Uncertainty - HB Gelatt
7. Career Satisfaction & Success – B. Haldane
8. Gifts: Dependable Strengths for Your Future – B. Haldane & J. Haldane
9. Making Vocational Choices – John L. Holland
10. The New Retirement, Discovering Your Dream – Richard P. Johnson, PH.D
11. Character Strengths & Virtues – C. Peterson & M. Seligman
12. Authentic Happiness – Martin P. Seligman
13. I Could Do Anything if I Only Knew What it Was – B. Sher
14. Do What You Love, the Money Will Follow – M. Sinetar
15. 2 Young 2 Retire – Howard Stone

Chapter References

Chapter One:

Holland Code: Making Vocational Choices: A Theory of Careers 1985 / 1997, John Holland

Chapter Two:

The Law of Attraction – E. Hicks & J. Hicks 2006/7

Chapter Three:

a. *Zen and the Art of Making a Living – Lawrence Bolt*
b. *Wheel of Life: Paul Meyer founder of Success Motivation Institute www.success.com/profile/paul-j-meyer*
c. *Finding Your Perfect Work – Paul & Sara Edwards*
d. *Power Up Your Passions - Ann Ronan www.successnet.org / http://authenticlifeinstitute.com/*

Chapter Four:

a. *Values List - Co-Active Coaching 3rd edition – H. Kimsey House & Karen Kimsey House*
b. *Work Values Inventory – Adapted from Santa Cruz County ROP*

Chapter Five:

a. *Dependable Strengths – Bernard Haldane*
b. *Career Satisfaction and Success – Bernard Haldane / 1995*
c. *Character Strengths and Virtues Personal Strengths Inventory – Martin Seligman www.authentichappiness.com*

Chapter Six:

a. *Personal Excellence: Be Your Best Self, Live Your Best Life – Celestine Chua www.personalexcellence.com*

b. *Creative Decision Making 1995 – H.B. Gelatt*

c. *www.clovercoaching.com - Linda Markley*

Chapter Seven:

The Complete Job Search Handbook - Everything you need to know to get the job you want- Howard Figler, 1999

Chapter Eight:

Personality Checklist - Heidelberg College Handbook, www.heidelberg.edu 7/07

Pride List – University of Waterloo- Career Development Manual, 2001-2002

Chapter Nine:

a. *Retirement Options – Richard Johnson*

b. *Too Young to Retire – Howard Stone*

Chapter Ten:

What Color is Your Parachute – R. Bolles 2010

Chapter Eleven:

The Big Shift: Navigating the New Stage Beyond Mid–Life – M. Friedman

Chapter Twelve:

6 Steps to Fulfilling Work –Ann Ronan, Authentic Life Institute http://authenticlifeinstitute.com/ 2010

Appendix

a. *Three P's of Interviewing- www.campus-to-career.com*

ABOUT THE AUTHOR

At an early age, Halimah Bellows became aware of her natural ability to listen to people non-judgmentally as well as her desire to be of service to others. In her life as an educator, a career counselor and a coach, she has been able to marry her fascination with people's stories with her deep interest in the world of work.

After completing her undergraduate studies in Social Science and Education at New York University, Halimah went on to earn an MA in English Language Teaching at the University of Exeter in England and then taught English as a Second Language in England and Indonesia. Returning to the United States, she earned her MS in Counseling Psychology at San Francisco State University and received intensive Certified Coach Training at The Coaches Training Institute in San Rafael, California and Retirement Options in St. Louis, Missouri to become a Certified Retirement and Professional Coach. Additionally she has obtained graduate certificates in Training Systems Development and Educational Drama. She holds Washington and California Community College Teaching and Counseling Credentials and is a Certified Dependable Strengths Articulation Process Facilitator.

For more than 20 years, Halimah has been helping her clients champion their careers and find their ideal jobs. She has a special gift for gently but relentlessly sifting through the mist and fog of clients' experiences and impressions and bringing the clarity of their insights to light. Halimah is a seasoned workshop presenter and group facilitator and has led many seminars and retreats for a variety of educational institutions, religious groups, nonprofit organizations and corporations. She is the creator of CAREER QUEST CARDS ©TM, a practical, portable career-building tool providing a distillation of 30 key career-coaching exercises (now available as an app for android, iPhone, iPad or Kindle Fire).

Halimah has appeared as a guest on a number of local radio talk shows in the Pacific Northwest. In addition to assisting people through career transitions and supporting retirees to "retire with fire," she also focuses on helping couples and business partnerships build powerful intentional relationships as well as empowering artists, entrepreneurs and professionals to develop their businesses and achieve their dreams.

FOR COUNSELING, COACHING OR PRESENTATIONS, contact:

championyourcareer@gmail.com, hbellows@careerquestcards.com or hbellows@championyourcareer.com. or (206) 595-7927.